WELFARE AND RATIONAL CARE

⫸MP⫷

PRINCETON MONOGRAPHS

IN PHILOSOPHY

⁋MP

The Princeton Monographs in Philosophy series
offers short historical and systematic studies
on a wide variety of philosophical topics.

Justice Is Conflict, by STUART HAMPSHIRE

Self-Deception Unmasked, by ALFRED R. MELE

Liberty Worth the Name, by GIDEON YAFFE

Public Goods, Private Goods, by RAYMOND GEUSS

Welfare and Rational Care, by STEPHEN DARWALL

WELFARE AND RATIONAL CARE

Stephen Darwall

PRINCETON UNIVERSITY PRESS

PRINCETON AND OXFORD

Library of Congress Cataloging-in-Publication Data

Darwall, Stephen L., 1946–
Welfare and rational care / Stephen Darwall.
p. cm.—(Princeton monographs in philosophy)
Includes bibliographical references (p.) and index.
ISBN 0-691-09252-4 (alk. paper)
1. Ethics. 2. Contentment. I. Title. II. Series.
BJ1012.D335 2002
177′.7—dc21   2002019845

British Library Cataloging-in-Publication Data available.

This book has been composed in Janson and Centaur Display

Printed on acid-free paper.∞

www.pup.princeton.edu

Printed in the United States of America

1 3 5 7 9 10 8 6 4 2

For Rosemarie

Contents

Acknowledgments

THE IDEAS presented here were stimulated by a conversation I had about ten years ago over coffee with Elizabeth Anderson. I had been reading the manuscript of Anderson's *Value in Ethics and Economics* and had been struck by her claim that we value the state of realizing someone's welfare because we care for that individual and so value *her* in a distinctive way. Surely, I had thought, caring for someone just *is* wanting her welfare. I accepted the Kantian doctrine that respect is a distinctive attitude toward a person rather than a state, but I hadn't seen that this is also true of what I here call sympathetic concern or care. Over the course of that conversation, Liz convinced me that I had been wrong.

Slowly the idea began to grow in me that if that were right, then perhaps the very idea of a person's good or welfare could itself be understood in terms of what one should want for someone insofar as one cares for her or, equivalently, what one should want for her for her sake. This is the rational care theory of welfare that I defend in this book.

In writing it, I have incurred many debts. Philosophically, I have drawn most, as I say, from Anderson and, as well, from David Velleman, as will be evident from the notes. I have also been much helped by Allan Gibbard's views about normativity and normative judgment, and Peter Railton's ideas have been a model for me of the best in naturalist approaches. I owe a great deal as well to other Michigan colleagues and to many current and former Michigan graduate students with whom I have discussed these ideas, including Jeff Brand-Ballard, Justin D'Arms, Ted Hinchman, Dan Jacobson, Katie McShane, Connie Rosati, Nishi Shah, David Sobel, Peter Vranas, and Andrea Westlund.

Chapters II and IV are based on essays that were initially written for conferences organized by the Social Philosophy & Policy Center at Bowling Green State University. I am grateful to Fred Miller, Jeff Paul, and Ellen Frankel Paul for organizing those conferences, to the participants for very valuable discussion, and to colleagues at various institutions where this material was also presented. Among these, I am especially indebted to Richard Arneson, David Brink, and Tom Hurka, as well as to David Copp, Tom Hill, Tito Magri, Michael Slote, Susan Wolf, and the late Jean Hampton. I am grateful also to the editors of *Social Philosophy & Policy*, and especially, to Ellen Frankel Paul, for editorial help with these two essays, and for permission to reprint material from them here ("Self-Interest and Self-Concern," *Social Philosophy & Policy* 14 [1997]: 158–178; Valuing Activity," *Social Philosophy & Policy* 16 [1999]: 176–196.).

Chapter III is based on an essay that was initially prepared for a symposium on altruism with Philip Kitcher at the 1997 Pacific Division Meetings of the American Philosophical Association in Berkeley, California. I am thankful to Philip Kitcher and members of the audience for their comments, especially to Arthur Kuflik. The essay was published under the title "Empathy, Sympathy,

Care" (*Philosophical Studies* 89 [1998]: 261–282). I thank the editors and Kluwer Academic Publishers for kind permission to reprint some of that material here. I am also very indebted to Linda Rosier for permission to reprint the photograph of David Golub that appears on page 74.

Tom Hurka and an anonymous referee read the manuscript for Princeton University Press and made many helpful suggestions. Finally, many thanks to Harry Frankfurt and to Ian Malcolm at the Press for their help.

WELFARE AND RATIONAL CARE

—————————•ꟼMꟼ•—————————

I

Welfare's Normativity

THIS BOOK concerns what we variously call a person's good, interest, well-being, or welfare: the good of a person in the sense of what benefits *her*.[1] This differs, I shall argue, from what a person herself values, prefers, or takes an interest in, even rationally. It is true, of course, that helping someone realize her values is almost always a significant part of advancing her welfare. Still, a person's good is a different thing from what she holds good, either actually or rationally, even from her own point of view.

One way to see this is to think about what it is to care for someone. When we care for a person, we desire his good for its own sake, not just as a means to other ends. But not for *its* sake only (that is, for his good's sake). Any desire for another's good that springs from concern for that person is also for *his* sake. The object of care is the individual person himself.

Desires are usually individuated by their objects, which are identified with states of affairs. But a desire for someone's good rooted in care has, in addition to the "direct" object of the person's good or the state of its being realized, an "indirect" object: the person himself.[2] We desire his good *for his sake*.

To appreciate what these last three words add, consider that it seems possible for an intrinsic desire for someone's

welfare to arise through the sort of associative process by
which Mill explains the genesis of an intrinsic desire for
wealth, or even, perhaps, through whim or fancy, without
involving any concern for the person himself.[3] Mill claims
that people come to desire wealth even when it lacks instrumental value because of its psychological associations
with other things they intrinsically desire. Were a desire
for someone's good to arise similarly, it might involve no
concern whatsoever for the person himself. One might
simply desire intrinsically *that* another's good be realized
without desiring this for *his* sake.

Caring for someone involves a whole complex of emotions, sensitivities, and dispositions to attend in ways that
a simple desire that another be benefited need not. If
someone about whom I care is miserable and suffering, I
will be disposed to emotional responses, for example, to
sadness on his behalf, that cannot be explained by the
mere fact that an intrinsic desire for his welfare is not
realized. Taken by itself, all that would explain would be
dissatisfaction, disappointment, or frustration.

Consider now the difference between the perspective
we take when, in caring for someone, we attempt to work
out what is good for her, on the one hand, and the perspective that is implicit in her own values, interests, and
preferences, on the other. The former is a perspective we
attempt to take *on* the person, whereas the person's own
values are what seems good to her from *her* point of view.

Of course, a person can have concern for herself,
and to the extent that she does, she will be the object of
her own regard. She will have herself and her good in
view. From her perspective what seems valuable will then
include herself and her own welfare. But it is virtually
unimaginable that a person's concerns could be exhausted

by self-concern, or even by what would satisfy it. There will inevitable be things whose value seems different to her from her own viewpoint than they do when filtered through the lens of self-regard. Indeed, it is entirely conceivable, maybe even commonplace, that a person can care relatively little for herself and her own welfare. Sometimes this will just be because other things matter much more to her. But it can also happen, in depression, for example, that someone cares little for herself because she seems to herself not to be worth caring much about.

The difference between empathy and sympathy is instructive here. Empathy is the imaginative occupying of another's viewpoint, seeing and feeling things as we imagine her to see and feel them. Sympathy for someone, on the other hand, is felt, not as from her standpoint, but as from the perspective of someone (anyone) caring for her.[4] Empathizing with someone in a deep depression, we imagine how things feel to her, for example, how worthless she feels. When, however, we view her situation with sympathy (a sympathy she perhaps can't muster for herself), she and her welfare seem important, not worthless.

Another reflection of the difference between a person's good and what is, or seems, good from his point of view is the possibility of pursuing values one cares deeply about at some cost to oneself. If there were no difference between what a person valued and what benefited him, self-sacrifice would be impossible, except through weakness of will. Pursuing some values at the cost of others would be possible, of course. But it would be impossible for pursuing one's values ever to cost one *on balance*, since realizing a value would be the same thing as benefiting from it.[5] I shall argue, however, that we should distinguish between how much a person values or takes an interest in something (or would rationally do so), on the one hand, and its benefit *to him* or contribution to *his* good, welfare, or interest, on the other. Much of life, I believe, involves investments that are warranted, even in one's own view, by values that bear no direct proportionality to personal benefit. Some things I attempt to provide my children, for example, will bear fruit, if ever, only decades after I am dead and no longer in a position to be benefited much by anything. Still, even though a person's good and what is good from his point of view are two distinct things, I shall also argue that we frequently promote the first by promoting the second.

Care and the Normativity of Welfare

I shall be claiming that a person's good is constituted, not by what that person values, prefers, or wants (or should value), but by what one (perhaps she) should want *insofar as one cares about her*. Partly, this will involve a claim about what kind of *normativity* the concept of welfare possesses. It seems to be widely accepted that welfare is a normative notion in the sense that an 'ought' or normative reasons claim follows from the proposition that something is for someone's good. Usually, this is because it is believed that if something is for my good, then it follows that I ought, or have reason, to want or pursue it. It is assumed, that is, that welfare has an *agent-relative* normativity, that a person's welfare is necessarily normative for *his own* desires and actions.

If a person's welfare were the same thing as apparent or actual good from her own point of view—what the person values or has reason to value—then it would have this agent-relative normativity. To value something is to see it as giving one reasons. From the agent's point of view, values bring reasons and warrant for desire and action in their wake. Of course, a person's values may be unwarranted or otherwise mistaken. What she takes to give her reason may not actually justify her desires and acts. But they do give her reasons in her own view, at least. And if her values are warranted, they give her reasons in fact.

As we have noted, however, it seems possible for a person to place relatively low value on herself and her own welfare. For example, she might care much more about specific projects, people, groups, or institutions she is related or committed to in various ways. Now I shall argue in Chapter IV that activities in which we realize and appreciate significant values are an important source of personal benefit. But that doesn't make a person's values the same thing as her welfare. Even though realizing and appreciating values benefits one, the values realized and appreciated are distinct from the benefit *to one* that comes through realizing and appreciating them. And caring about the values, or the specific things valued, is not the same as caring about the benefit that one's relation to these values can bring. It seems entirely possible to be passionately and enthusiastically devoted to values and to care relatively little about the benefits *one* gains by realizing or appreciating them.

More dramatically, someone may not value his own welfare because, in a depression, he sees himself as *unworthy* of care or even, perhaps, because he loathes himself. Depression or self-loathing doesn't entirely extinguish values and preferences, however. The depressive may prefer isolation and sleep, even though he knows that he might enjoy and benefit more from going out with friends: "Sure, that would be better for *me*," he might say, "but why does that matter? Why think I am worth caring for?" And the self-loather might take the fact that he would benefit from an activity as a reason *not* to engage in it. To both, the thesis that one's own good or welfare entails reasons for acting will seem to mock the truth.

Most would agree, of course, that the depressive and the self-loather are mistaken in thinking that considerations of their own welfare give them no reasons. But what these characters think isn't self-contradictory or conceptually incoherent. And because it isn't, the normativity of welfare cannot consist in entailing agent-relative reasons for the person's own desires and actions. The notion that, as one is unworthy, one's good gives one no reasons, is not the incoherent thought that what is (as one thinks) valuable, gives one no reasons. It is *conceptually* possible that considerations of one's own good provide no normative reasons for acting whatsoever or even, as the self-loather believes, that they provide "counter" reasons. To claim otherwise, as I assume we would, is to put forward a substantive normative thesis, not an analytic or conceptual truth.

To understand the normativity of welfare, I shall argue, we must see it in relation to care. What the depressive is right about is that if he weren't worth caring for, considerations of his own good would not be reasons. It's just that he is wrong in thinking he is unworthy of care. The deep truth that underlies the depressive's claim is that it is a person's being worthy of concern (as he will seem to someone who actually cares for him) that makes considerations of his welfare into reasons. What *is* a conceptual truth is that to care for someone is to be in a relation to him such that considerations of that person's welfare are normative for one's desires and actions with respect to him. *What is for someone's good or welfare is what one ought to desire and promote insofar as one cares for him.*

In this respect, the normative relation between care and welfare has a similar status to that of the familiar principle of instrumental reasoning that underlies hypothetical imperatives, namely, that insofar as one aims at an end, one ought (must) take the "indispensably necessary" means that are in one's power.[6] Kant plausibly claims that this normative principle is guaranteed to be true by the concepts of ends and means. To adopt an end is to place oneself under a norm of consistency requiring that one either take the necessary means or renounce the end. Similarly, caring for someone involves a normative relation to that person's welfare. Insofar as one cares for someone, one ought to be guided by the person's good in one's desires and actions.

If we take it only this far, however, welfare's normativity will seem only hypothetical in the same way means/end reasoning is. The consistency constraint that governs means and ends requires only that one either take the necessary means *or* give up the end. It neither puts forward a "categorical" normative reason for taking the means that is conditional on having adopted the relevant end, nor puts forward the fact of having adopted that end as a categorical reason for taking the relevant means. From the facts that one has adopted A as end and that B is a necessary means to A, it does not follow that one ought or has reason to do B.[7] If one had no reason to adopt A (or worse, reason not to do so), then maybe one should not do B, but give up A. The reasons it puts forward are conditional, not on the fact of having a given end, but, as it were, on a normative "hypothesis" that one accepts or is committed to in having the end—namely, that the end is to be, or ought to be, accomplished.[8]

Caring for someone places one under a similar consistency constraint of being guided by that person's welfare. Welfare is normative for care. Insofar as we care for someone, we ought to be guided by his good.[9] So far, these reasons are merely hypothetical. The idea, however, is not that the fact that one cares about someone makes considerations of his good reasons for one. The reasons are not conditional on one's caring. If that were so, they would be canceled once one ceased to care. They are conditional, rather, on a hypothesis one accepts or is committed to *in* caring, namely, that the cared for is *worth* caring for.[10] I shall argue in Chapter III that sympathetic concern partly involves seeing the person for whom one cares as having value himself, as being someone worth caring for.[11] What gives considerations of someone's welfare or personal good the status of normative reasons is his having a value that makes him worthy of care, as one accepts when one cares for him.

A Rational Care Theory of Welfare

So far we have that the normativity of welfare must be understood in relation to a concern for someone for that person's sake. I will be claiming, in addition, that a stronger relation exists between welfare and care, namely, that what it is for something to be good for someone *just is* for it to be something one should desire for him for his sake, that is, insofar as one cares for him. The relevant sense of 'should' again, is its most general normative sense. We might equivalently say that what it is for something to be good for someone is for it to be something that is rational (makes sense, is warranted or justified) to desire for him insofar as one cares about him. This is a *rational care theory of welfare*. It says that being (part of) someone's welfare is being something that it would be rational to want for him for his sake.

This might seem to get the relation between care and welfare backward. Surely, it will be said, it is welfare that is the independent variable here and rational care the dependent variable. Concern for someone just is a sensitivity to his good. Unless facts about welfare are fixed independently of concern, how will concern have, as it were, anything to be responsive to?[12]

As a useful analogy, consider the relationship between belief and truth. Beliefs are sometimes said to have truth as a "constitutive aim."[13] It is the nature of beliefs that they aim to be true, to be sensitive to the facts. The point is not just that they have what Hume called a "representative quality," that they represent some proposition *as* true.[14] When we imagine that *p*, or assume that *p*, we also represent *p* as true, even if we don't believe it. The idea is that beliefs are *regulated* by truth in a way that imaginings or assumptions are not. Truth is normative for belief. It is of the nature of beliefs that they *ought* to be true. If a representing that *p* is utterly insensitive to evidence of *p*'s truth, then we are apt to discount it as a genuine belief and consider it a representational state of some less committed kind.

Similarly, it might be thought, welfare is normative for care. It is simply part of what it is to care for someone, that it is regulated by the welfare of the person cared for. If I care about someone, then I ought to desire what is good for that person.

In the case of belief, we can distinguish between a formal and a substantive aim.[15] Belief's formal aim is to believe what we ought to believe. Its substantive aim is to believe what is true. By satisfying belief's substantive aim, we satisfy its formal aim. We believe what we ought to believe by believing what is true, or what is most likely to be true given our evidence. The sense in which truth is a substantive, and not a merely formal, aim is that truth is a distinct concept from the normative concept of what we ought to believe. That we ought to believe what is true differs from the tautology that we ought to believe what we ought to believe. For this reason, it seems a mistake to try to understand truth in terms of what we ought to believe. Wouldn't it involve a similar mistake to try to understand welfare in terms of what we ought to desire for someone's sake? This would leave us with the tautology that we ought to desire for someone's sake is what we ought to desire for his sake.

I believe that the claim that what we ought to desire for someone's sake is what is good for him *is* a tautology. Welfare is not simply normative for care in the way that truth is normative for belief. Rather, welfare is the same concept or thing as what is normative for care in the way I have indicated. To say that truth is a substantive, rather than formal, aim for belief is to say that, although truth is normative for belief, the concept of truth is not itself an explicitly normative concept, in particular, that it differs from the concept of what we ought to believe. If a person's good were to play an analogous role in relation to concern and desires for someone's sake, then it too would have to be a non-normative concept that differs from the concept of what we ought to desire for someone's sake. But this is not the case. Welfare is a normative concept and, as I shall argue, there is no other plausible normative concept for it to be other than that of what we should desire for someone's sake.

In particular, it seems possible for two people who care about someone, S, to coherently disagree about whether something, X, is good for S, even though they agree completely about all the non-normative facts concerning X and S. If the concept of a person's good were like the concept of truth in the relevant respect, this should not be possible. Two people cannot agree on all the non-normative facts concerning p—for example, they cannot agree that p—and still coherently disagree about whether p is true. And since truth is belief's substantive aim, they cannot agree about p and p's truth, and coherently disagree about whether they should believe p.[16] It does seem possible, however, for two people to disagree about whether X is good for S, even if they are completely agreed on every non-normative fact concerning X and S.

Suppose, for example, that X is a pleasant illusory belief of S's, say, that S's novel has sold 10,000 copies (when in fact it has sold only 12). It would seem that two people could be agreed about everything else, but simply disagree about whether this pleasant illusory belief is good for S or makes some contribution to his welfare, other things being equal. In such a case, it is hard to see what else they could be disagreeing about other than whether X is to be (ought to be) desired for S's sake, or, equivalently, whether it would be rational (warranted, justified, make sense) for someone who cared about S to desire X for S.[17]

If this is right, then welfare is not just normative for care in the way that truth is normative for belief. Rather, welfare must be an explicitly normative concept. My pro-

posal will be that it is the concept of what we would
rationally desire for someone insofar as we care for her,
or, equivalently, what is rational to desire for her for
her sake.

This is the view—a rational care theory of welfare—
that I defend in this book. It is a position in the metaethics
of welfare concerning the concept of a person's good or
what it is for something to be good for someone. It thus
differs from normative theories of welfare, either of what
things are good for us or of what *makes* a person's life go
better for her. It differs, that is, both from a theory of
what has prudential value and from a theory of what are
"prudential value-makers."[18] It is a metaethical theory of
the concept of someone's good or of what it is for something to be good for someone, have prudential value, be
in his interest, or be part of his welfare.

If, however, being normative for care or desires for
someone's sake is part of the concept of welfare, how then
are we to identify care or concern? Obviously care cannot
be *defined* in terms of welfare on pain of circularity. But a
rational care theory of welfare doesn't require a definition
of care. It is enough if care or concern exists as a natural
psychological kind for us to refer to. In Chapter III, I
argue that this is the case. A review of recent psychological literature on empathy and sympathy suggests that nor-
mal human beings have a psychological mechanism, one
I call sympathetic concern, that is distinct from, but related to, empathy in its various forms. If concern or care
for someone for his sake is a natural psychological kind,
then we can make use of it in a theory of welfare without
having to define it.

To glimpse the plausibility of this idea, consider the
relation between caring for someone and desiring his

good. Even if we cannot define what it is to care for someone, we can still grasp the way care or concern enters into
psychological explanations. For example, we can appreciate how someone might desire someone else's good *because* he cares for her. And we can appreciate also how the
converse doesn't hold, that we never explain a person's
caring for someone by the fact that he or she desires that
person's good. There is an apparent explanatory asymme-
try here that is quite familiar to us even if we lack a definition of care. Moreover, we easily accept as explaining
someone's fear, joy, or sadness *for* someone the fact that
he cares for that person, and that the presence of these
emotions cannot be explained by the mere failure of an
intrinsic desire for his welfare to be satisfied.[19] Even if we
have no definition of caring for someone for his own sake,
I shall argue, it is sufficiently evident to us that there is
such a psychological state for us to make use of it in a
rational care theory of welfare.

I should stress that care of concern *for* someone (or
something) for his (its) sake can differ from other kinds
of care or concern. There is a broad sense in which we
can be said to care *about* anything just in case we value
it.[20] But something's being important or making a difference to one in this broad sense need not involve
care or concern *for* any person or thing, whether we think
it objectively important or just important to us. Someone might care intensely and wholeheartedly about
whether his shirts are ironed without this involving any
concern for anything for *its* sake, including the shirts.
The kind of care or concern that is involved in a rational
care theory of welfare is concern for someone for the
person's sake.

Care and Respect

Neither is caring for a person, in the sense in which we shall be interested, the only way of valuing a person intrinsically, in or for herself. We can speak of doing things for someone's sake or on her behalf, when what we have in mind is respect rather than care. Making this distinction is another way of appreciating the difference between what is good from an agent's point of view and what is for her good or welfare.

Like care, respect takes the person herself as object. But whereas caring for someone involves relating to her as a being with a welfare, respecting someone entails relating to her as a being with a dignity. Insofar as we care for someone, we want what is good for her. Insofar as we respect someone, we regulate our conduct toward her by her dignity. And whereas the concept of welfare, I am arguing, is that of what we should want for a being for her own sake, the concept of dignity is that of a nexus of normative constraints on choice and action deriving from someone's (or something's) being the kind of being she (or it) is.[21]

Reasons for acting that are rooted in respect are both agent-regarding and agent-relative. First, respect for persons is a responsiveness to what makes them persons, the capacity for free agency. What we must attend to here is not, primarily anyway, what is for someone's good, but what she holds good and would want from her point of view. We may rightly think that unhealthy habits are harmful for someone, but think as well that respect tells against exerting undue pressure to induce her to change. Second, respect's reasons are agent-relative. A person's own values and preferences give *her* reasons to realize and promote them, and *others* reasons to permit her to do so, whether or not the resulting states are good from an agent-neutral point of view.[22]

Reasons of care, on the other hard, are welfare-regarding and agent-neutral. From the perspective of "one caring,"[23] the cared for's values are regulative only insofar as they are represented in his welfare or good. Of course, they very frequently are, but they generate reasons of care only to the extent that they are. Moreover, to one caring, considerations of welfare present themselves as agent-neutral, rather than agent-relative. From the perspective of sympathetic concern, what benefits the cared for seems not only good for him; it seems a good thing absolutely (agent-neutrally) that he benefited in this way.

Think of a parent's relation to his child at different stages of life. A toddler's desires and will give normative reasons to a parent just insofar as they indicate or represent what is for the child's good. If the child doesn't want to eat his broccoli, then this fact may have no independent weight, except insofar as it indicates that it will be frustrating, painful, and so on, to the child to do so. When, however, the child matures into a competent agent, then his will and desires do acquire independent weight. For a parent to be regulated only by his child's good at this point is paternalism in the pejorative sense.

The contrast between respect and care thus reconfirms the distinction between what is or seems good from someone's viewpoint and what is for his good or welfare. Treating another's point of view as normative is a form of respect. Taking a person's welfare as normative is a form of care. The respect we demand from others calls for empathy. The care we hope for, from some at least, is sympathy.

This contrast also helps to bring out a tension within the utilitarian tradition. Originally, the claim that morality is a matter of maximizing overall happiness was thought to derive from equal care or benevolence. For example, Francis Hutcheson, who first formulated the principle of the "greatest happiness for the greatest numbers" in English, grounded it in universal benevolence.[24] And theological utilitarians, like Berkeley, inferred utilitarian normative doctrines from a metaethical voluntarism combined with the doctrine of divine omnibenevolence.[25]

Usually these views were combined with hedonist theories of welfare. In the last century, however, it became more common to find utilitarianism formulated in terms of preference-satisfaction. Now if I am right about welfare, giving equal weight to each person's preferences or rational preferences, to what each values or should value, from his point of view, is not what one is led to by caring equally for every person or, perhaps, even more obviously, by caring equally for every sentient creature. If we put positivist scruples about access to subjective states to one side, therefore, preference forms of utilitarianism seem to be more sensibly grounded in what economists call "consumer sovereignty," that is, in some principle of equal respect, rather than universal benevolence or equal concern.

From Meta- to Normative Ethics: Welfare and Appreciating Values

After exploring the psychology of care in Chapter III, as one must to defend a rational care metaethics of welfare,

I turn in Chapter IV to the normative question of what makes a person's life go well and defend a version of the Aristotelian claim that the best life for a person, in the sense of that with the greatest prudential value or welfare, is a life of virtuous activity in something approaching the Aristotelian sense. This normative claim is, of course, somewhat independent of any metaethical theory of what welfare is or of what the concept involves. But only somewhat. Even if metaethics and normative ethics are concerned with distinct questions, a *philosophical ethics*, as I term it, must ultimately fit metaethical and normative ethical claims and arguments together into a satisfyingly coherent whole.[26]

The normative claim I shall defend is that the best life for a person (in terms of welfare) is one involving activities that bring her into an appreciative rapport with various forms of agent-neutral value, such as beauty, the worth of living beings, and so on. This normative claim tends to support a rational care metaethics of welfare, I shall argue, and to be supported by it in turn. Partly because the perspective of sympathetic concern is an agent-neutral standpoint distinct from the agent-relative perspectives of *both* the carer and the cared for, it should not be surprising that what it makes sense to desire for someone from that standpoint must be sensitive, not just to what seems good in agent-relative terms (to either the carer or the cared for), but to what seems good agent-neutrally. A rational care theory of welfare can therefore offer support to an Aristotelian normative ethical claim about the good life, and vice versa.

For Aristotle, virtuous actions are chosen for their own sake as *kalon* or fine. They have an intrinsic (agent-neutral) value or merit that is distinct from the contribution they make to *eudaimonia*, the agent's own good or welfare, and they are chosen for the sake of that value (as well as, Aristotle believes, for the sake of *eudaimonia*). This creates a puzzle. How can an activity be chosen for its own sake *and* as exemplifying an abstract (agent-neutral) value: merit or the fine? The key to solving this puzzle, I argue, is the notion of *appreciation*. There is a way of appreciatively engaging in valuable activities that involves an experienced rapport to the value as exemplified in particular activities. We come to appreciate the value of the activity through a distinctively evaluative mode of awareness we have toward the activity itself.

Consider, for example, what it is like to listen with full engagement and enjoyment to a deeply moving musical performance, say, Samuel Barber's "Knoxville: Summer of 1915." On the one hand, the object of one's enjoyment and regard is particular, the individual performance, composition, and performers one is listening to and the activity of listening to them. On the other, one's engagement with each (and all) of these, and with the activity of listening to them, involves an appreciating of it as instancing a distinctive kind of agent-neutral value. The experience is, of course, beneficial—it is good *for one*. But the benefit itself involves experiences that are *as of* values, the profound beauty of the music, for example, that are agent-neutral. More important for our present point, appreciative engagement brings one into a rapport with these values that one cannot have by merely accepting, or even knowing of their existence in some other, second-hand way.

The appreciated values differ from welfare or, indeed, I argue, from any other sort of agent- or person-relative value. The most profound and satisfying benefits to oneself, I claim, come in activities that bring one into a rapport with things whose worth or importance one appreciates as neither just *for* some individual (in the way that welfare is) nor *from* any individual's point of view (in the way that agent-relative value can be). When, for example, we listen to an especially satisfying performance of the Barber, we see it as exemplifying aesthetic values and the distinctive worth of music, which present themselves as, in principle, available to anyone.

Some of the forms of worth with the most significance in human life, moreover, are those involved in relationships of care and concern. It is not unusual for parents, for example, to say that raising their children has provided them with experiences that are among the most deeply satisfying of their lives. Part of the reason for this, I believe, is that these experiences include a profound appreciation of the worth of their individual children and, consequently, the value and significance that caring for them has.

Again, although these are claims of normative ethics, they tend to support the rational care metaethics of welfare I have sketched in this chapter and will develop in the next. When I think about what I would wish for my own children, it seems obvious to me that central to such a life are activities in which they appreciate the value of their own lives, in part, by virtue of their rapport with things they rightly see as having worth. From this point of view, it seems to matter both that they have the relevant experiences—that their lives *seem* valuable to them in these ways—*and* that their lives really do exemplify these values. Either without the other may still make a contribution to welfare, but the two together make a contribution that seems greater by far.

Welfare and Philosophical Ethics

It should not be surprising that metaethics and normative ethics, although formally distinct, can bear on each other in these ways. Surely it is no accident that hedonistic or preference-satisfaction versions of utilitarian normative theories tend to go together with varieties of metaethical naturalism, or that deontological normative views cluster with intuitionism or Kantian constructivism. In general, one or another normative view will seem more or less attractive depending on one's metaethics, and, sometimes, vice versa. A comprehensive philosophical ethics should attempt to work out a coherent ethical and philosophical outlook that integrates normative ethical theory and metaethics in a mutually supporting way.

This is no less true when it comes to views about welfare than it is with respect to other ethical areas. The attraction of preference-satisfaction *normative* theories of well-being, I believe, derives almost completely from confusion at the metaethical level about the normativity of welfare. Specifically, these normative theories are almost always based on the metaethical idea that a person's good has a normativity that is intrinsically *agent-relative*, entailing reasons for acting for the agent himself, but no one else. In my view, this is almost the reverse of the truth. The normativity of welfare is not agent-relative but agent-neutral. A person's good is intrinsically normative, not for the agent herself, but for anyone who cares for her, herself included. Once we make this shift at the metaethical level, preference-satisfaction normative theories of welfare lose their attraction. What will seem good *for* a person, viewed from the perspective of someone who cares for her, will be different from what seems good *to* her.

One area where this metaethical shift can have potentially significant normative consequences is in environmental ethics. If, for example, we can sensibly care about nonsentient biological species, or natural places, for their own sakes, then these will have a welfare, despite the fact that we cannot attribute desires or preferences to them.[27] Things will be good or bad *for* them, despite the fact that nothing can be good or bad *to* them.

II

Welfare and Care

There was no other explanation which seemed reasonable. . . . [W]as it not reasonable to assume that he meant never to claim his birthright? If this were so, what right had he, William Cecil Clayton, to thwart the wishes, to balk the self-sacrifice of this strange man? If Tarzan of the Apes could do this thing to save Jane Porter from unhappiness, why should he, to whose care she was intrusting her whole future, do aught to jeopardize her interests?

And so he reasoned until the first generous impulse to proclaim the truth and relinquish his titles and his estates to their rightful owner was forgotten beneath the mass of sophistries which self-interest had advanced.

—Edgar Rice Burroughs, *The Return of Tarzan*

Having found a telegram addressed to Tarzan with the news that Tarzan rather than he is the rightful Lord Greystoke, William Cecil Clayton ponders his future and the recent actions of "this strange man," Tarzan. Tarzan despairs, notwithstanding this recent news, of providing his beloved Jane the social place he believes her happiness requires. Worse, Jane is already promised to Clayton and would not permit herself to leave him, or, at least, to do so happily. So Tarzan decides to leave Jane with Clayton, thereby clearing her way to a happy life, although at the cost of his own happiness.[1]

As he marvels at Tarzan's self-sacrificing altruism, Clayton comes up with deliberations that are a mass of self-serving "sophistries." He acknowledges that Jane can never really be happy with him, since she loves Tarzan, and that he can assure Jane's happiness by relinquishing his social place to Tarzan, its rightful occupant, and releasing her from her promise. However, since he also believes that he would himself be better off with Jane, he persuades himself that it is only fitting that he live out the role Tarzan evidently intends for him.

The point of Burroughs's heavy-handed contrast is obvious enough. Clayton's self-deceit is a creature of civilized society, which demands that self-interested motivation be masked and indirect, laying low under rationalizations through which we self-servingly squelch naturally generous human motives. The ubiquity of masks, moreover, breeds cynicism about the very possibility of genuine other-concern, at least in polite society. Clayton can see Tarzan's leaving as self-sacrificial only because he regards Tarzan as a naïf, incapable of civilized sophistries. This gives Burroughs his final irony. In his admiration for Tarzan's noble self-sacrifice, Clayton finds the materials for his own self-serving rationalization.

But what *is* a person's good, welfare, or interest? And what claim does our own good make on us? These questions are interrelated. So long as the concept of a person's welfare is seen as having a normativity that is intrinsically agent-relative, as entailing normative reasons distinctively for the *agent's own* desires and actions, it will seem inevitable that welfare consists in whatever it makes sense for a person to want and, therefore, to attempt to realize. To a first approximation, what is *in* a person's interest will seem to consist in whatever an agent (rationally) *takes* an interest in. This, however, make self-sacrificial acts, such as Tarzan's appears to be, impossible. In valuing Jane's happiness and attempting to realize it by leaving her, Tarzan turns out necessarily to benefit himself, more, indeed, than he could by staying, regardless of whatever other apparently self-regarding reasons he might have for wanting to do so.[2]

My contrary claim is that a person's good, and the desire to promote it, are most naturally seen in relation to care or concern for a person for his own sake. A person's interest is not the set, or weighted sum, of things in which he takes an interest, either actually or rationally. These, we might say, are his actual or rational *interests*. The idea of person's good or *interest*—what is for his welfare or *in* his interest—is one we need insofar as we (or he) can care about *him*.

To care about a person is not to care about whatever that person cares about, or would rationally care about, even if the person in question is oneself. Appreciating this will lead us to a narrower view of welfare and link it less to a theory of rational desire and action than to something closer to ethical concern, since in caring about someone (another or ourselves) we see her good as giving reasons to anyone, or at least to anyone who can care.

A person's welfare is, I claim, the object of a desire spawned by concern for that person. Moreover, *self*-concern, as I shall also argue, is only incidentally egocentric. Unlike *de se* attitudes, its object is the individual one is rather than oneself as such. So self-concern is an instance, in one's own case, of an attitude one can have in principle toward any person.[3] It will follow that one's own good gives one reasons in the same way it can give them, agent-neutrally, to anyone, namely, from the perspective of concern for the person one is.

The Scope Problem and Informed-Desire Accounts of Welfare

I shall take it that a person's welfare is the same as any of the following: her interest, benefit, well-being, or good (her life's being good for her). Talk about a person's good or of something's being good for a person is ambiguous, however, and confusion often results from not keeping different meanings straight. We sometimes say that something is good *for* someone when we just mean that the person believes it to be or regards it as good. Plainly, this can differ from the person's own good or welfare. If I become convinced that the preservation of an endangered species is an intrinsically good thing that is not the same as concluding that I will benefit. There is, however, another sense of 'good for' that differs from colorless evaluative belief, which it is easier to confuse with welfare. This is the kind of holding good or dear, involving some personal stake and commitment, that we are apt to have in mind when we talk about "personal values." I shall argue, however, that this too differs from welfare. Tarzan clearly has a personal stake in Jane's welfare, but even if he were right about Clayton, it wouldn't follow that realizing this personal value of Tarzan's would add to Tarzan's welfare.[4]

In addition to these different senses of 'good for' there is one last meaning of a 'good life' that we need to distinguish. 'A good life' may refer to the life that *benefits* the person most, in which her life goes best *for her*. Or it may refer to a *worthy* life for the person, a life of merit or worth. Whether a person's life is good for or benefits her, I shall argue, is a matter of whether it is desirable for her sake, whether it would make sense to desire it out of concern for *her*. Whether a life has merit, on the other hand, consists in its being *estimable* or admirable, and its having worth involves its mattering or having significance or importance.[5] Of course, one may desire for someone's sake that her life have merit or worth. Indeed, I shall argue in Chapter IV that this is an important element of welfare. But that doesn't make merit or worth the same thing as welfare.

So what is a person's good or welfare? In the past thirty years a number of philosophers have followed what they have taken to be Sidgwick's lead in identifying it as the (ideal) object of the person's informed desires.[6] Sidgwick's own normative theory of good was hedonistic, but there seems little doubt that a significant attraction of informed-desire accounts has been their ability to vindicate the widespread sense that human welfare goes beyond subjective experience while preserving the subjective element of prudential value as what is valuable *to the person himself*. If, on reflection, it matters to us that our lives be real rather than the output of an experience machine, for example, informed-desire accounts can underwrite our sense that the former really is better (for us). As in Griffin's example of Freud, who preferred to spend his last days in torment rather than in a drug-induced euphoric confusion, it seems quite plausible that enduring even painful reality can sometimes really be for our good.[7] An informed-desire theory can explain why this is so.

At the same time, it seems unacceptably broad to include within a person's welfare whatever he wants when fully informed, as Tarzan's example shows. We may call this the "scope problem." Assumably, Tarzan prefers on reflection to leave Jane with Clayton, but Burroughs clearly does not want us to infer that this would be best *for Tarzan*, or that Tarzan should believe that it is. If that were so, leaving Jane would not be self-sacrificial. It would be doing what would most advance his own good, as well as Jane's.[8]

An example from Derek Parfit makes the point even more strikingly.[9] If, after an affecting conversation with a stranger whom you will never hear of again, you form a desire for her welfare, the satisfaction of that desire years later and unbeknownst to you does not add to *your* welfare.

Informed-desire accounts face objections on other fronts as well. One problem concerns temporal perspective. The time of something whose value for the person is in question may be well enough fixed, but what point in the person's life do we fix on to idealize her desires in order to determine the thing's benefit for her? If I want to know whether it would be for my good to go to a concert a year from now, do I ask, What, if I were to know everything (including how it will then seem to me), would I want now for then? Or do I ask, What would I then want for then? Or are facts about welfare somehow relative to the temporal perspective of an agent deliberating about how to promote his good?

A second issue concerns the difference between what a fully knowledgeable me would want in my circumstances and what a fully knowledgeable me would want for me in my circumstances as I actually am. How can it benefit me to do what I *would* want were I fully knowledgeable and experienced if my relatively benighted state prevents me from appreciating the benefits that a fully knowledgeable and experienced me would realize?[10] Or conversely, it may plainly be good for me to acquire information that a fully knowledgeable me would already have. What is for my good cannot therefore be what I would want if fully knowledgeable. To avoid this problem, an informed-desire account should be formulated in the way Peter Railton does, as what I would, if fully knowledgeable, want for myself as I actually am.

Let us set aside these two problems, however, to focus on the scope problem. Mark Overvold has suggested the following restriction to deal with this issue. In order for the satisfaction of a(n informed) desire to add to a person's welfare, the person must himself be an "essential constituent" of the desired state of affairs. More specifically, in order for a desired outcome (at t) to constitute a benefit to that person, the person's own existence (at t) must be a logically necessary condition of the outcome's obtaining (at t).[11] This restricts outcomes that can positively or negatively affect someone's welfare to those within her own life. Since the object of Tarzan's desire that Jane be happy does not essentially involve him, its satisfaction does not count toward his welfare. And similarly for the desire for the once-met stranger's welfare in Parfit's example.

Greg Kavka has argued against Overvold's restriction that it would exclude such self-interested desires as the desire for posthumous fame. Were someone to neglect her duties in order to advance such an aim, Kavka points out, "we wouldn't hesitate to characterize it as selfish."[12] But desires may be selfish without being such that their satisfaction is for a person's good.[13] For example, an action may be both selfish and self-destructive, as the all-too-familiar cases of men who kill their partners, children, and then themselves surely show.[14] So from the fact that the desire for posthumous fame can motivate selfish behavior, we shouldn't conclude that its satisfaction, even if informed, adds to a person's welfare.

Of course, there might be other reasons for objecting to Overvold's restriction. Although it seems possible for a desire for posthumous fame to be selfish without being self-interested, it might be self-interested nonetheless. Perhaps posthumous fame can make an intrinsic addition to a person's welfare. We must remember, however, that the issue is not whether posthumous fame is something it can make sense for a person to care about, but whether its realization *benefits the person*. Self-sacrificial cases such as Tarzan's show we must distinguish these two issues. Once we separate them, it may be hard to see how things entirely beyond the boundaries of a person's life *can* benefit or harm that person intrinsically, how they can make an intrinsic difference in the value of life *for that person*.[15]

Let us take it provisionally, therefore, that any plausible informed-desire account of welfare would have to accept something like Overvold's restriction as a necessary condition. Combining the two as a putative sufficient condition generates an informed-desire version of what Parfit has called the *success theory*: something is for a person's good if it advances what that person would (informedly) desire *for her life*.[16] How plausible is this theory? Again, the question is not whether it would make sense for a person to *take an interest* in whatever she would informedly desire for her life, but whether whatever satisfies this condition is thereby *in* her interest in the sense of being something that *benefits her* or makes her life go better *for her*.[17]

To see that it is not, consider Jane's situation. As Burroughs represents her, Jane's greatest desire is to do her duty. Having promised to marry Clayton, she believes she must ultimately do so (although she allows herself to believe that she may put him off for a while). Of course, Jane wishes desperately that she hadn't promised herself to Clayton and gotten into this situation. But there it is; she has. And what she wants most to do in her situation as she sees it (on what she takes to be good evidence) is to do her duty and marry Clayton. Moreover, her desire to do her duty is both intrinsic and one whose object concerns her own life. But that hardly makes it the case that she will benefit by marrying Clayton, that this will promote *her* welfare. Of course, it may be for her good nonetheless. For example, maybe (as Tarzan believes) she would be so miserable if she broke her promise that, in the circumstances, duty and interest coincide. But that would not be simply because her duty matters more to her than other things, but because of what her life would be like were she to break, or keep, her promise.

This is only one example of a wide variety of desires that are intrinsic and that satisfy the Overvold restriction, but whose realization is not related in any principled way to the person's welfare. In many such cases, it seems certain that the desire's satisfaction does not contribute to the person's good to a degree proportional to its strength, and arguable that its satisfaction is not for the person's welfare at all. Consider a consuming passion for contemporaneous fame. A person may know what such fame would be like and still desire it wildly out of proportion to any real benefit. The object of his desire unquestionably matters a great deal *to* him, but may nonetheless not be particularly good *for* him, although, of course, it may be. In such cases, I am inclined to think, what matters most to the person is not what *would* matter most to him if he cared more about himself.

The key to understanding the concept of welfare, I believe, is to see its connection to caring and concern. A person's welfare is what we want promoted insofar as we care about that person.[18] If, consequently, any informed-desire standard can serve as a plausible criterion of welfare, I think it will be something like the following. Something is for someone's good if it is what that person would want for herself, as she actually is, insofar as she is fully knowledgeable and experienced *and* unreservedly concerned for herself.

Sidgwick's Account

I shall consider some consequences of this suggestion later. At this point, however, I want to approach our problem from a different angle, by investigating Sidgwick's influential account of a person's good. Actually, Sidgwick gives several different formulations, and it is instructive to compare these. He begins with:

> (1) [Something is desirable for a person if it is] what would be desired [by that person], with strength proportioned to the degree of desirability, if it were judged attainable by voluntary action, supposing the desirer to have a perfect forecast, emotional as well as intellectual, of the state of attainment or fruition. (ME.111)

A consequence of (1), Sidgwick believes, is:

> (1)' [M]y good on the whole is what I should actually de-
> sire and seek if all the consequences of seeking it could be
> foreknown and adequately realised by me in imagination
> at the time of making the choice. (ME.111)

Sidgwick argues that (1) and (1)' are inadequate because
they are insufficiently attentive to comparisons and opportunity costs. Someone may be well enough satisfied
with something without its being for his good on the
whole, since it may make him relatively impervious to alternatives he might have preferred more. So Sidgwick
substitutes:

> (2) [A] man's good on the whole is what he would now
> desire and seek on the whole if all the consequences of all
> the different lines of conduct open to him were accurately
> seen and adequately realised in imagination at the present
> point in time. (ME.111–112)

With this classic formulation of Sidgwick's in hand, we
may now return to the "time of desire" issue we pre-
viously set aside. Notably, (1)' and (2) consider the question of what is for a person's good from the perspective
of an agent who is in a position to make choices that can
affect its realization. To determine whether it is for my
good to attend a concert a year from now I am to consider
what I would want *now for then* if I were fully informed,
including about what it would be like to attend the concert then.[19] This has a number of interesting consequences. Most strikingly, it appears to make facts about a
person's good relative to the standpoint of an agent considering whether to seek it. It is logically possible, for example, that even when preceded by fully informed and

imaginatively vivid consideration of the same facts and features, my desires with respect to the impending concert could change. And if so, then either there is no enduring fact of the matter about the contribution going to the concert on that date would make to my good, or any such facts are relative to an agent's choice context.

But why should the contribution that going to a concert a year from now would actually make to my good depend in any way on what I would want *now*, even were I to take fully into account what it would be like for me then? If we distinguish the issue of whether going to the concert would be *in* my interest from the question of whether it would make sense for me now to *take* an interest in going to the concert a year from now, it seems fairly clear that while what I would informedly want is arguably relevant to the latter question, it has no evident relevance to the former. (2) conflates these two issues.

We can see this more clearly by noting how Sidgwick goes on. He says of (2) that it proposes a deliberative ideal that "is entirely interpretable in terms of *fact*, actual or hypothetical, and does not introduce any judgment of value . . . still less any 'dictate of Reason'" (ME.112). Consequently, it leaves out a central normative aspect of the idea of a person's good as Sidgwick understands it, namely, that it is an end the person *ought* to seek. So Sidgwick suggests a substitute for (2), albeit one that "keep[s] the notion of 'dictate' or 'imperative' merely implicit and latent."

> (3) 'Ultimate good on the whole for me' [means] what I should practically desire if my desires were in harmony with reason, assuming my own existence alone to be considered. (ME.112)

The relative clause, "assuming my own existence alone to be considered," is a fascinating addition, to which we shall return presently. The point I wish now to make is that Sidgwick evidently treats it as an adequacy condition on an account of a person's good that it secure what he takes to be its necessary practical relevance to the agent's deliberative standpoint at earlier times. To count as an adequate account of a person's good, a theory must ensure that what it reckons to be in a person's interest is something in which reason dictates he take an interest (including at all earlier times when it is at stake).

Something like this movement of thought, I believe, lies behind the acceptance of informed-desire theories of welfare, generally. What an agent can herself be brought to desire through improved knowledge, experience, or imagination is an "internal reason" in Williams's sense.[20] Informed-desire theories thus promise an account of interest that appears to guarantee that if something is in our interest, we have reason to take an interest in it. They apparently guarantee, that is, an *agent-relative* normativity of the agent's welfare, namely, for *the agent's own* choice and action.

Nevertheless, whatever plausibility informed-desire theories have as theories of rational choice, of what it is rational for an agent to *take an interest in*, may not be preserved when we consider them as accounts of what is *in a person's interest* or for her welfare. While it is plausible to hold that going to a concert a year from now can be something it is rational for me to take an interest in now only if there exists some practical connection to my current deliberative standpoint, it is simply not obvious why this should be necessary for it to be true that some future occurrence *will* benefit me or be for my welfare. Whether it would benefit me to go to a concert a year from now would seem not to depend on anything about my deliberative perspective now. So far as I can see, when we have established that some future action would be for my welfare, it is still a logically open question whether that is something it is rational for me to take an interest in now.

Of course, we might, as a semantic matter, simply use 'welfare' to refer to whatever is useful in promoting the agent's current desires, her rational desires, or some subset of these. But if we do, we will lose the conceptual connection between welfare and benefit, which is apparently not deliberation-relative.[21] The benefits of going to a concert a year hence do not accrue to me now (or to me-now), no matter how much I now care, or rationally, about going then.[22]

Sidgwick is a hedonist. So he believes that the best life for a person is whichever offers her the most pleasure in the long run. But whether my going to a concert a year from now would be hedonistically optimal doesn't depend on my current choice context. So why does Sidgwick think that what I would ideally want now is whatever would turn out to be hedonistically optimal for me overall? Formulation (3) provides the key. My good is what I would desire "if my desires were *in harmony with reason*" (ME.112, emphasis added). Sidgwick asumes that a person's good has agent-relative normativity, and he believes that it never makes sense for someone to want something other than a pleasurable experience.[23] If, consequently, my desires with respect to future experiences are out of proportion to the pleasure I expect from them—for example, if I care less now about the pleasures of a concert a year in the future than I do about other, more proximate things—then either my proximate desires take things other than pleasurable consciousness as object, which Sidgwick believes they cannot rationally do, or they conflict with "an equal regard for all the moments of our conscious experience . . . [that] is an essential characteristic of rational conduct" (ME.111).

In earlier editions of the *Methods*, Sidgwick brings hedonism more directly into his definition of welfare:

> (2)' [W]hat he would desire on the whole if all the consequences of all the different lines of conduct open to him were *actually exercising on him an impulsive force proportioned to the desires or aversions which they would excite if actually experienced.*[24]

From Sidgwick's account of pleasure as desirable consciousness together with his belief that we would desire nothing on reflection except (desirable) consciousness, it will follow that a person's good lies along the "line of conduct" that promises the most pleasure. (2)' is effectively a procedural version of the "equal regard" constraint, interpreted in the light of hedonism.

To conclude our investigation of Sidgwick's account, I want to note two important elements that those who draw from him frequently ignore. First, as we observed briefly in passing above, in addition to including an explicit restriction to rational desires, Sidgwick's definition of a person's good is also restricted to desires that concern only the person himself. A person's good is what that person would desire were his desires "in harmony with reason, *assuming [his] own existence alone to be considered*" (ME.112, emphasis added).

More important, and second, even before Sidgwick states formula (1), he restricts it to what a person desires both intrinsically ("for itself") and "*for himself—not benev-*

olently for others" (ME.109, emphasis added). This second restriction is especially signficant in light of the connection I have claimed between welfare and care. If we take Sidgwick literally here, we have to interpret a desire *for oneself*, not simply as a desire *with respect to oneself*, but as the analogue in one's own case of benevolence, something that could motivate action *for one's own sake*. This effectively restricts Sidgwick's informed-desire theory of a person's good to desires whose objects are desired out of a self-*concern* that is analogous to benevolence.

I hope it is plausible by now that this restriction is well-motivated. If the notion of rational or informed desire is to enter into an account of welfare, it will not be through the idea of what that person would sensibly desire, even with respect just to herself, but through some notion of what someone who cared for her (perhaps she herself) would sensibly desire *for her(self)*, that is, for her sake.

Now it is central to the way Sidgwick sees things that a person's own good necessarily makes a rational claim on that person. Nothing can count as an adequate account of a person's good, he thinks, unless it secures the rational dictate for *the agent himself* to promote it. But so far as I can see, practical reason includes no intrinsic requirement that we care either about others or about ourselves, since rational agency seems possible without even the capacity to care about a person, oneself or others, for that person's sake.[25] Because I regard the self-concern restriction as well-motivated, however, I draw the conclusion that there is no fundamental rational requirement to promote one's own good on the whole.[26] Welfare's normativity is not agent-relative.

Rather, there is a "hypothetical" requirement that one be guided by a person's (one's own) welfare insofar as one cares about that person (oneself). This requirement is hypothetical in the same sense as the more familiar requirement of instrumental rationality (when properly understood). The point is not that one should (categorically) be guided by one's own good on the condition that one cares about oneself. Rather, insofar as one cares about oneself, one is committed to accepting a "hypothesis" (that one is worth caring about), and the rational dictate to promote one's own good is conditional on that.[27]

Others may agree with me that practical reason does not dictate either self-concern or benevolence, but want to preserve a basic connection between a person's welfare and what that person has reason to do. This will require them, however, to reject a connection between welfare and concern for a person for his sake (and to accept a conception of welfare on which self-sacrifice is conceptually problematic). I turn next, therefore, to the question of whether there is some rational requirement to pursue one's good on the whole.

Welfare and Rational Choice

Sidgwick is a hedonist about welfare *and* about what it makes sense for a person to value and desire. I believe that is why he thinks that a person's good necessarily makes a rational claim on her.

But why must these two views go together? Why couldn't hedonism be true as a normative theory of welfare, but false as a normative theory of rational desire and choice? I am not suggesting that hedonism *is* true as a theory of welfare. It does, however, seem more plausible as an account of welfare than it does as a theory of rational desire and choice. The very idea of welfare, as we've said, is of a value that accrues to and exists in benefiting some individual. And if, like Sidgwick, one thinks of pleasures as experiences or feelings that are "apprehended as desirable by the sentient individual at the time of feeling it," a welfare hedonism may seem a natural conclusion (ME.129).

But this progression of thought requires no view whatsoever concerning whether one's own (future) good, so conceived, necessarily makes a rational claim on one in deliberating about what to do. One could be led to a welfare hedonism on these grounds while holding steadfastly to some version of what Parfit calls a "present-aim theory" of rational choice, for example. Thus I might simultaneously think that it would be for my good to go to a concert a year from now, because it would give me pleasure, but also believe that this makes no significant rational claim on my current deliberations if, on reflection, I care relatively little about myself and my welfare.

Moreover, not all objections to a hedonist theory of rational choice obviously apply to a hedonism of welfare. For example, Jane thinks she should marry Clayton because she has promised to do so. She thinks not just that it would be morally wrong in some externalist sense to fail to marry him, but that there is decisive reason for her to do so. We can imagine that she also thinks that this has nothing to do with considerations of anyone's pleasure, and, therefore, that she would reject a hedonist theory of rational choice. But this would not commit her to rejecting a hedonist theory of welfare. One could be a hedonist about welfare while holding that all sorts of things—ideals, norms, moral principles, projects, aesthetic or religious conceptions, and so on—that cannot be understood hedonistically make a rational claim in deliberation. Indeed, one could be a hedonist about welfare and deny that considerations of welfare have *any* intrinsic normativity for the agent's own choices.

The fact that hedonism can have an appeal as a normative theory of welfare that does not transfer to a hedonist theory of rational choice shows that we do well to separate these two matters at the metaethical level. We should not follow Sidgwick's lead in supposing that something cannot count as an adequate metaethical theory of welfare unless it secures a rational claim to promote it.

One thing that separates the question of what it is rational for a person to choose or do from the issue of what is for her good is the "internalism requirement." Philosophers with different fundamental commitments—both Humeans and Kantians, for instance—find it a plausible constraint on what can make a rational claim on an agent that it be something that can engage her practically in deliberation.[28] Unless a consideration is one by which an agent would be motivated were she to take account of it rationally, it can give her no reason to act. To be a reason for her, a consideration must be something *on* which she could (autonomously) act.

What makes the internalist requirement a plausible constraint on a theory of rational choice has to do with the nature of reasons *for acting* and their essential connection to deliberation from the agent's point of view. But when it comes to the question of a person's welfare, these features seem not to be in play. Indeed, a being can have a welfare without being an agent at all. Sidgwick to the contrary, therefore, there seems to be nothing in the very idea of a person's welfare or good that guarantees any rational dictate to promote it.

Parfit has argued, partly along similar lines, that some version of a present-aim theory is a more plausible theory of rational choice than is a self-interest theory.[29] This may appear not to cut against Sidgwick, however, since what Parfit calls a *critical* present-aim theory *could* hold that the only desires that survive *rational* reflection (that are "in harmony with reason") are those for one's own good on the whole (or for pleasure more generally).[30] To put it differently, there is a way of interpreting the internalism requirement such that a proponent of the self-interest theory can claim his theory satisfies it just by virtue of claiming that the desire for one's greatest good is inherently rational. Interpreted this way, however, the internalism requirement has no teeth. Any considerations put forward as reasons can be held to satisfy it, since it can always be said that an agent would be motivated by them *if rational* (that is, if she were adequately responsive to reasons).[31]

To interpret the internalism requirement properly, we need to distinguish dependent from independent variables. Once we allow a substantive view of reasons to drive our standard of rational reflection, we risk a toothless internalism. The internalism requirement should therefore be understood to hold that in order to be a reason for someone to act, a consideration must be something she would be moved by on rational reflection, where what counts as rational reflection is not itself determined by some independent theory of reasons (such as the self-interest theory). Internalists should therefore favor what Parfit calls a "deliberative" rather than a critical version of the present-aim theory.[32]

One thing at issue between present-aim and self-interest theories of rational choice concerns temporal context.

According to deliberative present-aim theories, anything
that makes a rational claim must have some practical relevance to the agent's deliberation at the time of choice.
But again, there seems no reason to suppose that what is
for a person's good must meet such a condition. Whether
it would promote my welfare to attend a concert a year
hence seems to be one question. And, if it would benefit
me, whether that gives me a reason now to take an interest
in attending then seems to be another. Only the second
question, it seems, requires practical connection to the
agent's deliberative perspective.

Now Sidgwick allows that one might sensibly query,
from the present perspective, whether there is reason to
do what would be for one's good on the whole. But he
formulates the challenge this way: "Why should I sacrifice
a present pleasure for a greater one in the future?"
(ME.418). And he evidently thinks it a serious challenge
only for those who hold Humean views of the self and
personal identity (ME.419). But this way of posing the
challenge already assumes (better, insinuates) a form of
egoism, namely, what Parfit calls "hedonistic egoism of
the present."[33] Rather than asking what necessarily connects long-run self-interest to an agent's rational concerns (as required by a present-aim theory), it queries the
relation of long-run welfare to a particular concern (to
have pleasure now), whose rational standing it insinuates.
Posed in this way, the challenge can reasonably be met.[34]
If the problem is simply to justify a sacrifice of some present good *for oneself*, then it is surely enough to say that it
is to procure some greater good for oneself in the future,
which will more than compensate the sacrifice. Only tem-
porally extended beings can be benefited or harmed, so
the present and the future are merely different times at

which one can be benefited, not the locations of different beneficiaries, me-now versus me-then.[35] The real challenge to the self-interest theory comes, as Parfit argues, not from an egoism of the present moment, but from the present-aim theory.

Self-Interest and Self-Concern

Let us return now to viewing self-interest or welfare from the perspective of self-concern. We can begin with an example to illustrate that although concern for a person gives rise to a desire for her welfare, it is not similarly related to a desire for outcomes that *she* desires, even rationally. Suppose your friend Sheila is in the following situation. By donating all her disposable wealth she can realize an outcome she cares very much about, say, the rebuilding of a city ravaged by war to a certain degree, D. But there is a catch. Sheila also has a degenerative disease, which, if it is not checked, will create memory loss and confusion severe enough so that she will be unsure where her money has gone and unable even to hold stable beliefs about the state of rebuilding in the war-ravaged city. Happily, there is a relatively inexpensive drug that can arrest the symptoms of Sheila's disease without side effects. However, the drug is not free, Sheila will not accept donations, and she cares so much about rebuilding the city that, even though the difference the cost of the drug would make in the rebuilding effort is quite small (call it d), she nonetheless wants (and would continue to want on reflection) to forego the drug and donate all she has.

Sheila ranks the outcome of the city's being rebuilt to degree D together with her advanced disease, memory loss, and uncertainty about the city's actual state (call this outcome O_1) higher than the outcome of the city's being rebuilt to degree $D-d$ but with her knowing about the rebuilding, her role in it, and a generally improved mental state (call this outcome O_2). You are convinced that Sheila prefers O_1 to O_2, and that this ordering of outcomes would survive reflection. You care for Sheila and so desire what is for her good. Does caring for her and wanting her welfare dictate your ordering these outcomes in the same way Sheila does, even on reflection? It seems obvious that it does not. Although Sheila prefers O_1 to O_2, this in no way requires you to do so also insofar as you care for her. On the contrary, insofar as you care for Sheila and what is for *her* good, wouldn't your ordering be the opposite of hers? Wouldn't you prefer O_2 to O_1? (Notice, by the way, that while the quality of Sheila's experience in these two outcomes probably plays a significant role in your ordering of them, insofar as you care about her, it need not be the only factor. In O_2, Sheila would *know* about the city's improved state and her role in it.)

Of course, even if you would prefer O_2 to O_1 insofar as you care about Sheila, this wouldn't entail that you should subvert her wishes. As I mentioned in Chapter I, there is another way of valuing a person for herself, namely, respecting her (in the recognitional sense), that is different from care for a person for her own sake. And respecting Sheila will argue for respecting her wishes even though concern for her and her welfare tugs in a different direction.[36]

Now the scope problem arises for informed-preference views of welfare independently of any thought about the relation between welfare and concern for a person for her sake. Tarzan's example shows that. We sense a gap between options Tarzan rationally prefers and what would most benefit him. What Sheila's example shows is that the proposal that welfare is related to care in the way I have proposed can explain why such a gap should exist. If what it is for something to be for Sheila's good is for it to make sense for someone who cares for her to desire it for her sake, then if Sheila's ranking and that of someone who cares for her were to diverge in this way, this would explain why even though Sheila rationally prefers O_1 to O_2, O_2 is nonetheless better for her than O_1 in the sense of being more for her good or welfare.

Of course, this is not the only possible explanation of the gap. But a *rational care theory of welfare* has virtues that other explanations do not have. For example, metaethical hedonisms and objective list accounts, which hold that welfare is the same thing as pleasure or being on a list of "goods," also entail that what is for a person's good can diverge from what she prefers, actually or rationally. But these alternatives seem unable to capture the *normativity* that is intrinsic to the very idea of welfare. We can know that something will give pleasure or that it is on the list and still coherently (if misguidedly) ask why this creates normative reasons. Even if the question has an obvious answer, it is logically or conceptually open. If, however, a person's welfare just *is* whatever it makes sense for someone who cares for that person to want for her for her sake, then normativity is built in. The normativity is not, however, the agent-relative kind of rational preference. It is rather an agent-neutral normativity grasped from the perspective of someone who cares for the person.

As we noted in Chapter I, it seems possible for two individuals to agree about every non-normative fact that could possibly be relevant to a given welfare claim and still coherently disagree about the welfare claim.[37] For example, it seems possible for two individuals to disagree about whether a certain kind of pleasure makes a contribution to someone's good even if these individuals are in complete agreement about every potentially relevant non-normative fact. Perhaps one thinks that pleasure always adds to welfare, and the other denies this, holding that, say, pleasures based on false beliefs make no contribution. The remaining disagreement would appear to concern a normative question of some kind, but of exactly which kind?

The reflections of the previous section show that it is not the question of what *the agent* has reason or ought to do. One can agree that something would make a contribution to one's own welfare, but coherently (if, perhaps, mistakenly) deny that this gives one any reason to bring it about. A rational care theory explains how such normative disagreements about welfare are possible, since it interprets them as concerning what ought to be desired for that person for his sake, that is, insofar as one cares for him. When these individuals disagree about whether pleasure always makes a contribution to welfare, the normative question on which they are disagreed is whether every kind of pleasure is such that we ought to desire it for that person's sake, that is, out of concern for him.

According to the rational care theory, a person's welfare makes a normative claim on any person who cares for him for his own sake.[38] A rational care theory of welfare is thus able to explain all three of the following: (i) why welfare does not have the agent-relative normativity that rational-desire theories of welfare mistakenly suppose, (ii) why a gap exists between what is for a person's good and what he prefers or rationally prefers, and (iii) why welfare is nonetheless a normative notion, making a rational claim on anyone who cares about the person.

Despite these virtues, a rational care theory may still seem problematic. Don't we need to understand the idea of welfare first before we can understand what care is? This might be true if caring for someone were the same thing as desiring his good, but it is not. In the next chapter I shall argue that we can locate concern for a person for that person's sake within a naturalistic human psychology in a way that makes it available for use in a rational care theory of welfare. It is a reflection of this that although the fact that a person cares for someone can explain why she desires his welfare, the reverse is never true. We never explain someone's caring for another by pointing to the person's desire for the other's good. And as we noted in Chapter I, there can be intrinsic desires for someone's welfare that are entirely unrelated to care or a desire to benefit him for *his sake*.[39] Whatever its more specific structure, caring for someone seems to be related to a whole complex of forms of emotional engagement, sensitivity, and attention in ways that a simple desire that another be benefited need not be.

When we care for someone we desire things for her *for her sake*. The object of care is the person *herself*, not some state or property involving her.[40] In caring for her, we, of course, want certain states and properties involving her to be realized. But when they derive from care, such desires also have an "indirect object" in addition to these direct objects. In caring for her, we want these things *for her*. This does not mean just that we want the properties and states to involve her, as opposed to someone else. Or even that the desires are to be understood *de re* rather than *de dicto*. We want them for her *for her sake*.

There is, of course, much to be learned about the nature of care, but the phenomenon is familiar enough, as are many of its parameters. We know, for example, that we are more likely to care about someone when we engage her and her situation empathically, and that the reverse process holds as well. And even if we don't know very much about what care is, we may know it when we see it. For a rational care theory of welfare, it is enough that there be facts of the matter about whether someone cares for a person that are independent of any fact about welfare. And enough for us to be able to put the theory to use that we can recognize instances of caring.

A rational care theory of welfare does not, of course, hold that someone who cares for another can simply make it true that something is for that person's good just by desiring it for him for his sake. In order for a thing to be in a person's interest it must be something someone who cared about the person would *rationally* want for him for his sake.

Rational care theories can be neutral on which theory of rationality and rational desire is correct, but they must hold that there being nonrelative facts about welfare depend on there being facts about what anyone who cares for that person would rationally want for him, insofar as she cares. If something is good for someone in this sense, this makes no agent-relative claim on the agent that it does not make on others. Rather, anyone who cares for that person (the agent himself or someone else) will have reason to want it for his sake (consistently with this concern). Again, the idea is not that the reasons of welfare that are acknowledged by one who cares are conditional on the fact that one cares. Rather, caring involves seeing the cared for as worthy of care and, consequently, involves seeing their welfare as giving (agent-neutrally) reasons to anyone.

In caring for oneself in a way that spawns the desire to promote one's good *for one's sake*, one sees oneself as care-worthy, and one's welfare as reason-giving on this account. Such self-concern is not, it is important to appreciate, an attitude *de se*. If I care for myself and am, unbeknownst to me, the only philosopher to have played Little League in College Station, Texas, then I care for the person who satisfies this arcane description. In caring, one values oneself, and one's interest, not *as oneself* (that is, the valuer) but as the particular individual one happens to be and, hence, from a third-person perspective one can share with anyone (who can care). Reasons of welfare, rooted in care, are thus agent-neutral rather than agent-relative.

III

Empathy, Sympathy, Care

> No man is devoid of a heart sensitive to the suffering of others. . . . Suppose a man were, all of a sudden, to see a young child on the verge of falling into a well. He would certainly be moved to compassion.
> —MENCIUS

IN THIS CHAPTER, we turn to the question of how to understand and identify the attitude that is featured in a rational care theory of welfare. This confronts us with the worry that it is impossible to define care or concern without already making use of the idea of a person's good or welfare, and therefore that we cannot define welfare in terms of rational care. However, we need not define care (or, as I will call it in this chapter, sympathetic concern), if it is something like a psychological natural kind. Just as we can use a term like 'water' without a prior definition to refer to the natural stuff in the rivers and lakes for purposes of empirical theory, so likewise might we refer to care for purposes of a metaethical theory of welfare if it is a natural kind. I shall try to make this idea plausible in the current chapter by considering the psychology of sympathetic concern in relation to empathy in its various forms.

What Mencius's translator calls compassion in the passage above is an instance of what I shall call *sympathetic concern* or *sympathy*. It is a feeling or emotion that (i) responds to some apparent obstacle to an individual's welfare, (ii) has that individual himself as object, and (iii) involves concern for him, and thus for his welfare, for his sake. Seeing the child on the verge of falling, one is concerned for his safety, not just for its (his safety's) sake, but for *his* sake. One is concerned for *him*. Sympathy for the child is a way of caring for (and about) him.

Sympathy differs in this respect from several distinct psychological phenomena usually collected under the term 'empathy' that may involve no such concern. What these phenomena have in common is their involving feelings that are "congruent with the other's emotional state or condition," as one psychologist puts it.[1] Here it is the way things seem from the other's standpoint that is salient, in this case, the prospect of falling down the well. Empathy consists in feeling what one imagines he feels, or perhaps should feel (fear, say), or in some imagined copy of these feelings, whether one comes thereby to be concerned for the child or not. Empathy can be followed by the indifference of pure observation or even the cruelty of sadism. It all depends on why one is interested in the other's perspective.[2] Sympathy, on the other hand, is felt, not as from the child's perspective, but as from the perspective of "one caring."

We now know a good deal about the psychology of empathy and sympathy. Much of this was gleaned by earlier observers like Hume and Adam Smith, who correctly believed these emotional mechanisms to be central to human thought and practice.[3] But a large amount has come in the past hundred years, as experimental psychology has developed and theoretical speculations about empathy and sympathy have been submitted to experimental tests. In fact, 'empathy' was only coined in 1909 by Edward Titchener to translate Theodor Lipps's *'Einfühlung'*, which he in turn had appropriated for psychology from German aesthetics in 1905, and which derives from a verb meaning "to feel one's way into."[4] Both Hume and Smith had used 'sympathy' to refer to the distinctive forms of empathy they described.

It is obvious and uncontroversial that sympathetic concern for a person involves some concern for her good and some desire to promote it. My claim, again, is that the concept of welfare is one we need insofar as we are capable of care and sympathetic concern. Welfare is normative for care in the sense that it is intrinsic to the very idea of a person's good that threats to it are what it makes sense to be concerned about for that person for her sake.

In Chapters I and II, I argued that welfare has no conceptual connection to normative reasons from the first-person point of view of a rational agent.[5] It is neither conceptually nor metaphysically necessary (i) that whatever it makes sense for a person to desire and seek will contribute to his welfare, nor (ii) that whatever will advance his good is something he should rationally seek, even prima facie. Of course, we believe that any human being does have reason to be concerned about his own good. But what stands behind that belief? Why does it make sense for any person to be concerned about his own good?

According to some views of welfare, informed-desire accounts, for example, (ii) is true because (i) is: all and only what a person has reason to desire counts as part of his welfare.[6] The problem with these theories, however, is that they make rational self-sacrifice conceptually or metaphysically impossible. And they make rational egoism conceptually or metaphysically necessary rather than a substantive, indeed controversial, normative claim.

There are many things I rationally take an interest in, such as the survival of the planet and the happiness of my children long after I am dead, that will make no contribution to my welfare. A person may have rational *interests* that go well beyond what is for her good or *in her interest*. A person's good—what benefits her or advances her welfare—is different from what is good from her point of view or standpoint. The latter is the perspective of what she herself cares about, whereas her own good is what is desirable from the perspective of someone (perhaps she herself) who cares for her.

We have reason to care about our good, therefore, because we have reason to care about *ourselves*. A person's good is what it makes sense to want for that person's sake, that is, insofar as one cares about her.

If this is so, the primary locus of the concept of welfare is not a first-person agent's point of view, but the third-person perspective of one caring, a perspective we can take on ourselves no less than on others. I have reason to care about others' goods insofar as I have reason to care for them, and I have reason to care about my own good insofar as I have reason to care for myself. And while individuals may have more reason to care for themselves or close relations than they do for strangers, neither is possible without the (third-person) capacity to care for oneself *or* others that is involved in sympathetic concern.[7]

Empathy

To work toward a better insight into the psychological mechanisms involved in sympathetic concern, we should begin by distinguishing different forms of empathy. Whereas sympathy for a person and her plight is felt as from the third-person perspective of one caring, empathy involves something like a sharing of the other's mental states, frequently, as from her standpoint. This is different from caring for her, even imaginatively. After all, the person we are empathizing with may hate herself, think she is worthless, and want nothing more than the misery she believes she so richly deserves. Imaginatively sharing these concerns *of* hers (as first-personally) is hardly the same thing as sympathy *for* her.[8]

EMOTIONAL CONTAGION

The most rudimentary form of empathy is "emotional contagion" or "infection," as when one "catches" a feeling or emotional state from another, not by imaginative projection, but more directly.[9] Walking into a room filled with laughter and convivial conversation, we feel differently than when the room is filled with depression or with tension. This is a form of what Hume meant by "sympathy": the "propensity we have . . . to receive by communication [the] inclinations and sentiments" of others (T.316).[10]

Smiles and frowns (and yawns and coughs) beget their like, not because the person beholding a smiling face projects herself imaginatively into the smiler's standpoint and imagines what it would be like to be seeing things in that smiling way, but directly, without any mediating projective imaginative activity. Of course, Humean sympathy must be harnessed to the imagination to play the role Hume believes it does in moral judgment. Judging the merit of a character trait or motive, Hume thinks, we are carried by an association of ideas from thoughts of the trait or motive to thoughts of its usual effects, including of the pleasure or pain it tends to cause. But, as Hume understands it, sympathy has done no work yet. Its job in Hume's psychology is to take us from ideas of these pleasures or pains to pleasurable or painful feelings (Humean "impressions") and, thereby, to cause or constitute the moral sentiment that moral judgments express. Hume supposes that this happens directly, without any projection into the standpoint of those we imagine to be pleased or pained.[11]

Hume also believes, however, that emotional contagion functions through an "idea" of the communicated feeling. On his official theory, "sympathy" takes ideas of passions or feelings as inputs and transmits them into "the very passion[s]" themselves (T.317) by infusing them, more or less, with the impression of ourselves "that is always intimately present with us," the degree being determined by the psychological distance between the person whose feelings we are contemplating and ourselves. According to Hume, therefore, we must first be aware of feelings before sympathy can turn these into felt impressions. Hume to the contrary, however, we don't seem to require an idea of a contagious emotion to catch it. Being in the company of the anxious can create anxiety even in those who are unaware of it in their infectors.

How, then, does emotional contagion work? A central mechanism seems to be mimicry. Facial mimicry, which we now know to be present in neonates in their very first days, appears to be especially important.[12] But how can mimicry transfer feeling or emotion?

At least since Darwin, it has been noted that emotions correlate with specific bodily and facial movements.[13] Emotions whose bodily expressions are virtually universally recognized across cultures have been shown to include anger, disgust, contempt, sadness, grief, and happiness, among others.[14] So far, this just shows that distinctive feelings cause distinctive bodily expressions. Other studies, however, show that when subjects are directed to assume facial positions that are characteristic of an emotion without grasping the experimenter's ulterior purpose, they actually tend to experience the emotion themselves.[15] And subjects who are asked to pronounce phonemes involving muscle activity implicated in characteristic emotional facial expressions tend, when they comply, to feel those very feelings.[16] The facial expression produced by pronouncing the phoneme 'e', for example, resembles the smile. And it turns out that pronouncing 'e' leads to a happier feeling. There is more to saying "cheese" than we might have imagined.

Why all this should be is a fascinating question. Robert Zajonc hypothesizes that there is an afferent feedback system in which facial expression influences blood temperature in the brain, affecting serotonin levels and changing affect. Whatever the mechanism, there is impressive evidence that facial and other forms of motor mimicry produce feedback and that mimicry can tend not only to modulate, but also to initiate, felt emotion.

Another example of an apparently dedicated form of mimicry is the phenomenon of infant reactive crying. Studies have shown that neonates have a significant tendency to cry in reaction to tapes of crying infants of like age.[17] This "primary circular reaction" forms the first mode of Martin Hoffman's developmental theory of empathy. At this stage, empathic response in the child obviously involves no sense of the other as the primary locus of distress. Before they have any awareness of others as distinct individuals, children experience "global empathic distress," and are likely to seek comfort for themselves when other children cry.[18]

The hypothesis that motor mimicry is a major empathic mechanism was already present in Lipps's and Titchener's theories in the early 1900s. Experiments since have shown all manner of behaviors to evoke mimicry, including pain behavior, laughter, smiling, affection, embarrassment, discomfort, disgust, ducking, stuttering, word-finding, reaching, and success and failure at a timed task.[19]

There are fascinating experiments that tend to show that motor mimicry can also have a communicative function. When subjects witness apparent expressions of pain, their tendencies to mimic are substantially affected by how likely eye contact is with the pain-expressing person.[20] It is as if the function of empathic mimicry were to mirror the feelings of others. As the experimenters put it, "I show how you feel." Moreover, mimicry manifests "reflection symmetry." When two people are facing each other and one ducks to her right, the person facing her is likely to duck to his left.[21] In these instances, we mimic, not by stepping into others' shoes so much as by stepping into shoes that will mirror to them their expressive behavior in their shoes. This suggests a more interesting and satisfying mimetic basis for reciprocity (and, thus, reciprocal altruism) than mere copying. When *A* does something to *B*, reflection-symmetrical mimicry involves *B* doing the same to A *as* a reciprocation. Reflected mimicry supplies the target as well the behavior copied.

Emotional contagion is only a primitive form of empathy, involving no projection into the other's standpoint nor even, necessarily, any awareness of the other as a distinct self. When we share another's feelings through contagion, it is not "in her shoes," responding to her situation as we imagine she sees it.

Early on, however, infants begin to develop the rudiments of perspective taking that underlie more sophisticated forms of empathy. The relevant phenomena are "social referencing" and "joint visual attention." Young children have been shown experimentally to "reference" their mothers in potentially threatening circumstances, to check their attitude, and to modify their behavior in light of it.[22] As early as six months of age, babies in experiments whose mothers turn and direct their gaze to an object in another part of the room exhibit a tendency to turn also and fairly reliably discriminate the object to which their mothers are attending.[23] This is not the same thing as projection into the mother's perspective, but it certainly seems a movement toward it.

The difference between emotional contagion and "projective" empathy is something like the difference between Hume's "sympathy" and what Adam Smith refers to with the same term. Humean sympathy is felt as from an observer's standpoint, beginning with an idea of the other's feeling inferred as the cause of witnessed behavior. Smith argued, however, that the ability to form ideas of others' feelings already involves "sympathy" in his quite different sense. "By the imagination we place ourselves in [the other's] situation," and imagine "what we ourselves should feel in the like situation."[24] Smith's sympathy differs from Hume's in point of view and, consequently, in what it is about the other we have in view. "When we see a stroke aimed and just ready to fall upon the leg or arm of another person," Smith writes, "we naturally shrink and draw back our own leg or our own arm" (TMS.9). We respond to the other person's situation as from her standpoint rather than to her reaction or to an imagined version of it. And when the stroke falls, "we are hurt by it as well as the sufferer," if not in the same way (TMS.9). We feel an imagined surrogate of what the other actually feels.

Several philosophers of mind have recently argued that "simulation" of this kind is centrally involved in attributing mental states to others (much as Smith had claimed).[25] As against the "theory theory"—that we attribute mental states via a commonsense theory, inferring them as the best explanation of behavior, or by some induction over cases—these philosophers hold that we frequently simply simulate others and then attribute the simulated state. We place ourselves in their situation and work out what we would think, want, and do, if we were they. The idea is not that our thought is explicitly self-conscious: "If I were she, I would feel thus and so, so she probably feels thus and so." Rather, we unself-consciously project into the other's standpoint, respond imaginatively from that perspective, and attribute the result to the other.

To illustrate some evidence for simulation, consider the following story, with which subjects in a Kahneman and Tversky experiment were presented:

> Mr. Crane and Mr. Tees were scheduled to leave the airport on different flights, at the same time. They traveled

from town in the same limousine, were caught in a traffic
jam, and arrived at the airport 30 minutes after the scheduled departure time of their flights. Mr. Crane is told that
his flight left on time. Mr. Tees is told that his was delayed
and just left five minutes ago.[26]

Who is more upset? If you are like 96 percent of Kahneman and Tversky's subjects, you will answer: Mr. Tees.
How do we come to this conclusion? It seems implausible
to suppose we here survey generalizations or make induc-
tions about cases, and then attribute similar states by analogy. Rather, we apparently simply imagine ourselves in
the respective positions and attribute our imagined feelings to Mr. Crane and Mr. Tees. Better, we work out what
to feel from these perspectives, and attribute the results.
Thus, as Mr. Crane: "Oh well, I can't complain. After all,
that's when it was scheduled to go off." As Mr. Tees:
"Oooh, I hate it when that happens."[27]

It is important that projective empathy is not simply
copying others' feelings or thought processes as we imagine them. Rather, we place ourselves in the other's situation and work out what *to* feel, as though we were they.
This puts us into a position to *second* the other's feeling
or to dissent from it. As Smith puts it, we can thereby
express our sense of the "*propriety*" of the other's feeling,
whether, that is, we think it warranted or not. If we cannot
"enter into" an angry person's sense of a situation that
provokes her anger, we will feel her anger inappropriate
(TMS.11). Or if a person laments his misfortunes, but
"bringing [his] case home to ourselves" does not affect us
similarly, we will not share his grief but think it unwarranted (TMS.16).

There are two points worth emphasizing here. One,
which I will stress when we come to sympathy, is that

feelings present themselves *as warranted by features of the situation to which they apparently respond.* Fear involves seeing something as frightening, and so, as warranting fear. Disgust is as of the disgusting. And so on. From the perspective of a person having an emotion, one's situation presents itself as providing some warrant for the emotion. This doesn't mean that one must *believe* the emotion warranted, not even in any respect, and certainly not all things considered. Rather, things will *seem* to one as warranting the emotion (in something like the way the lines in the Müller-Lyer illusion seem to be of different length even to those who believe they are not).[28] It will be to one *as if* one's situation gave one reason to feel as one does.

The second point is that if one is inclined to believe that another's feelings are not warranted by her situation, this will make it more difficult to share them through projective empathy. Indeed, one's relative inability to empathize will itself be an expression of thinking the other's feelings to be unwarranted (in Smith's phrase, "improper"). When we do share others' feelings through projective empathy, consequently, we second and thereby confirm their feelings.

There are differences of degree here, of course. Sometimes we implicitly assess what more or less anyone would reasonably feel in the other's circumstances, as we presumably do when we attribute greater frustration to Mr. Tees and when we make Smithian judgments of propriety. On other occasions, we assess another's feelings more specifically in relation to her personal characteristics. This is the kind of projective empathy that is more appropriate to empathy *with* another, as when we share another's feeling as a way of caring (sympathetically) for her. "When I console with you for the loss of your only son,"

Smith writes, "in order to enter into your grief I do not consider what I, a person of such a character and profession, should suffer, if I had a son, and if that son were unfortunately to die: but I consider what I should suffer if I was really you, and I not only change circumstances with you, but I change persons and characters" (TMS.317). Empathy of this sort is closer to sympathy, since the grief I vicariously experience is "entirely upon your account, and not in the least upon my own" (TMS.317). So long, however, as my grief on your account is only as from your (unself-consciously) grief-stricken standpoint, and not from my standpoint in appreciation of yours, we have empathy without sympathy.[29]

Even when we project into others' characters, however, we must still be able to share their feelings as apparently warranted from that perspective. If we cannot see features of their situation as providing reasons for their emotions, we cannot share them. Here we are more likely to regard the other as, in this respect at least, more aptly the object of "objective" attitudes rather than the "participant reactive attitudes" that Strawson famously claimed are essential to common life.[30]

Projective empathy is thus no less communicative than Bavelas and her colleagues have found mimicry generally to be. When we projectively mirror others' feelings, we not only show them how they feel, we also indicate to them that we agree about how *to* feel. We show we understand their feelings and signal our willingness to participate with them in a common emotional life. This makes projective empathy central to the formation of normative communities—like-minded groups who can agree on norms of feeling. (Think here of post-1970s talk of the form: "I was like . . . , and he was like . . . , and I was like

..., and so on." Or: "He goes [some act displayed or described] and I go [some feeling displayed or described] ..." We might see these attempts to elicit projective empathy in interlocutors as ur-versions of fully articulate normative discussion about how to feel.)[31]

PROTO-SYMPATHETIC EMPATHY

Projective empathy is a projection into the other's standpoint. Attention is focused, not on the other, but on her situation as we imagine she sees it, or as we think she should see it. This, again, is a fundamental difference from sympathy. In sympathy, it is the other and the relevance of her situation *for her* that we focus on. There is, however, a form of empathy that brings these elements into view.

Consider the difference between the instructions: (i) imagine what someone would feel if he were to lose his only child, and (ii) imagine what it would be like for that person to feel that way. Complying with (i) involves simulating someone in the imagined circumstances in order to identify what feelings the situation would apparently warrant when so viewed. It need involve no attention at all to having those feelings or to suffering that loss. To comply with the second request, however, one would have to simulate, not just a person *with* the relevant feelings, but someone *conscious of* his feelings, their phenomenological textures, and their relevance for his life.

Call empathy of this latter form, *proto-sympathetic empathy*—"proto-sympathetic," because it brings the other's relation to his situation into view in a way that can engage sympathy on his behalf. A person grieves the loss of his child, and in sharing his grief projectively my focus is on the child who was lost, not on the person whose grief I share. When, however, I turn my attention to what it must be like to live with this loss, I focus on the person himself and the ways his grief pervades and affects his life. Before my thought was: What a terrible thing—a precious child is lost. Now my thought is: What a terrible thing for him—he has lost his precious child.

Proto-sympathetic empathy is informed by projective empathy, but goes beyond it in not being felt entirely as from the other's standpoint (or, at least, not without projected self-consciousness). Someone who has lost a child might be so consumed by the loss that he is unable even to think about what living with it is like for him. So someone simulating his experience would simulate being unable to either. Or perhaps the loss is so devastating that he denies it, thinking and acting as though the child were still alive. Only with the "double vision" provided by some perspective on the person and his feelings as well as by projective empathy with those very feelings can one imagine what life must be like for him.

Projective empathy involves imaginative (or "off-line") versions of the distress one imagines others to feel. Since Ezra Stotland's first experiments in 1969, however, studies have consistently shown that subjects who projectively empathize report actual emotions and show physical symptoms that parallel the likely reactions of their targets.[32] The imagined distress thus causes some level of real distress in the empathizers.

This distress can be felt as entirely personal. Martin Hoffman calls this "empathic distress," which he distinguishes from "sympathetic distress." Empathic distress has oneself as object and gives rise to efforts to comfort or relieve oneself. Sympathetic distress, on the other hand, has *another's* distress as object and tends to cause efforts on the other's behalf.[33] C. D. Batson and his colleagues make a similar distinction between "personal distress" and what they call genuine "empathy," including within the latter "other-focused . . . feelings of sympathy, compassion, [and] tenderness."[34]

As we are defining things, what Batson calls "empathy" is a form of sympathy. But we can see how proto-sympathetic empathy, at least, is significantly closer to Batson's "empathy" (that is, sympathy) than it is to personal distress. Like genuine sympathy, proto-sympathetic empathy has the other person and his plight as object. When we imagine what another person's grief is like for him, we are focused on the other person and his grief. And this means that the distress we feel vicariously by projective identification can find a new target, namely, *his* distress, thereby giving rise to sympathy. This new distress at his distress may be supported, moreover, by association with similar experiences we recall from our own lives. Recollecting one's own grief at losing a parent, say, may solidify one's sense of the other's loss and support a concern for the other by association with sympathy for oneself.

The point is not that proto-sympathetic empathy necessarily gives rise to sympathy. Someone in the grip of resentment, envy, or the desire for revenge may take delight in the vivid appreciation of another's plight he gets from imagining what another's situation must be like for her. However, when sympathy is blocked in such situations, it may be because empathic engagement is framed within some larger concern or narrative in which the other and her situation plays only a derivative role. If I see the other's plight as deserved, or as evidence of my own power, or as the plight of an enemy or competitor, then I am less likely to sympathize. But then I am not really attending undividedly to her or her plight. I am interested in her point of view only insofar as it enters into my own.

Sympathy

Over the past fifteen years, Batson and his colleagues have been finding experimental support for what they call the "Empathy-Altruism Hypothesis."[35] Because of the difference between Batson's definitions and ours, this research bears only indirectly on the relationship between empathy and sympathy as we are defining them. But the indirect light is pretty bright nonetheless.

Batson's experiments work by testing differences in the behavior of subjects who are given an opportunity to help someone they experience as being in need. The subjects are partitioned in two cross-cutting ways. One is a partitioning between "low empathy" and "high empathy" subjects. For example, some subjects might be told (as in Stotland's experiments) to imagine how the person they are observing feels (high empathy condition) with the rest being told to attend carefully to the information they learn from observing the person (low empathy). The other variable is "ease of escape," how easily subjects can avoid actually helping without retaining vicarious distress. In a wide range of experimental conditions, designed to rule out a wide variety of alternative hypotheses, high empathy subjects show a remarkable disposition to help others even when they can easily escape doing so without vicarious personal distress.

I take this as evidence of a psychological connection between empathy and sympathy in our terms. So far as I can see, all that is directly manipulated in Batson's experiments are forms of projective and proto-sympathetic empathy. Thus, when subjects are told to imagine what another person is feeling, they are being instructed to empathize, specifically, to engage in proto-sympathetic empathy, not to feel sympathy.

What Batson's subjects directly exhibit is helping behavior rather than sympathy. But Batson claims his experiments show that what explains this helping is a motivational state whose "ultimate goal" is "increasing the other's welfare."[36] I conjecture that, in many cases at least, this motivational state is sympathetic concern or sympathy.

Sympathy, again, is a feeling or emotion that responds to some apparent obstacle to an individual's good and involves concern for him, and thus for his welfare, for his sake. Introductory psychology students in one of Batson's early experiments hear an audiotape they believe to be of a fellow student, Carol, who has had to miss a month of class while hospitalized as the result of an auto accident. The subjects are asked if they will help Carol make up missed work. Subjects in the "difficult escape" condition are told that Carol will be back in their discussion section in a week, and those in the "easy escape" condition, that she will be studying at home, conveniently out of view. Subjects whose empathy is heightened by imagining what Carol must be feeling show a remarkable tendency to help, even in the easy escape condition (71 percent). Why?

Assume that Batson is right that his experiment shows that what moves these students is an other-directed rather than self-directed motive like the desire to remove vicarious personal distress. What is the nature of this other-directed motive? Of course, it might be that the subjects had some standing desire or principle to aid others in need and empathy simply makes Carol's need more evident than it would otherwise have been. Another, and I think more likely, possibility, is that the vicarious distress that high empathy subjects feel comes to have a new object, namely, Carol and her predicament. On this hypothesis, the subjects feel an emotion that is directed toward Carol and her plight. Their empathy gives rise to sympathy. Initially distressed, as from Carol's point of view, they came to be distressed *at* Carol's plight *and* on her behalf. They came to feel concern for her and, consequently, to desire relief from her plight *for her sake*.

SYMPATHY'S OBJECT

Sympathy is an individual-regarding emotion. We feel sympathy *for* someone, just as we can have fears or hopes for someone or on someone's behalf. All these emotions are forms of concern for a person for his own sake. The "for its sake" construction is revealing. Something is desired, felt, or done for something's "sake" when the desire, feeling, or action is out of *regard to (or for)*, that is, quite literally, with a view toward, that thing. It is with attention to or in consideration of the thing itself that we desire, feel, or act, when we do so for its sake.

According to philosophical orthodoxy, the standard object of desire, action, and feeling is some proposition or possible state of affairs. If I want an ice cream, the real object of my desire is that I eat an ice cream. Or if I fear a tiger, then perhaps I fear that I might be eaten by a tiger. Moreover, it sometimes seems implicit in ethical writing that what it is to care about another person is simply or primarily to have a desire with a specific propositional content, namely, that the person fare well.

Even if desires and feelings have propositional objects, however, some also have "indirect objects" that are non-propositional.[37] In particular, the form of desire involved in sympathetic concern does. Seeing the child on the verge of falling into the well, we don't simply desire that the disaster be averted. We desire this *for the child's sake*, that is, out of a sympathetic concern for *him*.

Notice the difference, again, between a desire that the child be safe and a desire for this for the child's sake. Virtually anything can strike our fancy. So we might imagine someone whimsically forming an intrinsic desire that the child be safe.[38] But a desire for this *for the child's sake* cannot be so formed, by its very nature. Any desire for something for someone's sake is a form of concern for that person and so not a matter of whimsy. Here we have a difference in desire that cannot be captured propositionally. Both desires have the same propositional object, but only the latter is a desire for that object for the child's sake. Either desire can motivate action for the goal or end of the child's safety, but only the latter can move us to seek this goal *for the child* or on the child's behalf.

SYMPATHY AND VALUE

Sympathy involves concern for another in light of apparent obstacles to her welfare. We desire her good, not just intrinsically (for *its* sake), but also for *hers*. Moreover, we do so in a way that connects us to values of two different kinds—welfare, or value *for her*, and agent-neutral value.

On the one hand, sympathy presents itself as warranted by potential obstacles to someone's good. Welfare is normative for sympathy. If a person's welfare is not at stake, then there is nothing to be concerned about on her behalf.

On the other hand, sympathetic concern presents itself as of, not just some harm or disvalue *to* another person, but also the *agent-neutral disvalue* of this personal harm owing to the value of the person himself. In feeling sympathy for the child, we perceive the impending disaster, not just as bad for him, but as neutrally bad, as bad *period*. Here the apparent disvalue seems to provide a reason for anyone to prevent it. It seems a bad thing absolutely that a child be harmed in this way. We experience the child's plight as mattering categorically because we experience the child as mattering.

The point is not that sympathy makes these claims true, or even that it counts as evidence for them. Rather, sympathy's emotional presentation is *as of* the neutral disvalue of another's woe, and hence, as of a categorical reason for preventing it. To the person sympathizing, it is as if there is a reason to relieve the other's suffering consisting simply in the fact that the person herself, and so her good, matters.

It is useful here again to compare sympathy with a whimsical (or an habitual) desire for someone's welfare. The latter desires might be intrinsic, the other's good being desired for its own sake and not just as a means to other goods. However, a whimsical desirer of another's welfare need not regard himself as having a categorical reason for furthering the other's good that is unconditional on his desiring it. If I whimsically desire do to something simply for its own sake, I won't see myself as having a reason to do so even in the hypothetical case in which I am not struck by that fancy. But this is precisely what seems to be involved from the perspective of someone feeling sympathy. We experience the threat to the child as a categorical reason for aid that is unconditional on our now wanting this. And if others deny the reason, that will conflict with the way it seems to us from our sympathetic perspective.

Sympathetic concern thus involves an experience (less committally, an appearance) of its objects, individual people, for example, and hence, of their welfare as mattering in a way that is not just agent-relative. If we credit these appearances in our own case, we will conclude that our welfare matters, not just *to us*, but categorically and agent-neutrally, because, as it seems to us when we are the objects of our own sympathetic concern, *we* matter categorically and agent-neutrally.[39]

On a rational care theory of welfare, we start with the idea of caring for someone for her own sake, an idea with which we are familiar from the phenomenon of sympathetic concern. And we then say that what it is for something to be good for that person is for there to be *reason* to want it for her (on her behalf, that is, insofar as one cares about her). In other words, what makes a desire other- or self-regarding is not that it is directed toward the relevant person's good, but that it springs from and expresses self- or other-*regard*, a concern *for that person*. And what makes something good for someone (self or other), is that it is the object of a rational self- or other-regarding desire. What is primitive is concern for the person. Something is good *for that person* by virtue of being something it makes sense for anyone caring about her (perhaps she herself) to want for her sake.

If some view along these lines is correct, then the concern we experience for people in sympathy is central, not just to seeing individuals and their well-being as having categorical importance, but also to the very concept of well-being or personal good. A person's good has intrinsic normative force, not for desire in general, not even for those of the person herself. Rather, personal welfare is normative for desires *for that person's sake*, and thus for concern for that person. It is because we can take up the standpoint of one caring toward ourselves and others and ask what it makes sense to want from that point of view that we have a need for the concept. When we take up that standpoint, moreover, and see the cared for as valuable, as worthy of care, we see her welfare as giving reasons, even, indeed, to those who do not care for her.

This chapter should give us some assurance that sympathetic concern is a natural psychological mechanism, one that is distinct from, but causally related to, empathy in its various forms. We may therefore take it that the phenomenon of care for someone for her own sake is available for metaethical theorizing, specifically, for a rational care theory of welfare.

IV

Valuing Activity: Golub's Smile

To THIS POINT, we have been concerned with the metaethics of welfare, with defending the rational care theory
and exhibiting the psychological characteristics of sympa-
thethic concern necessary for it to feature in such a theory. In this final chapter, we turn to the normative question of what kind of life is best for human beings in the
sense of benefiting them most or providing them the
greatest welfare.

Strictly speaking, questions of normative ethics are logically independent of metaethical issues, and this is no less
true when it comes to welfare. Virtually any combination
of metaethical and normative ethical positions on welfare
is logically possible, although it would be impossible, for
example, for nonsentient beings to be harmed if welfare
consisted (metaethically) in the satisfaction of desires.
Despite strict logical independence, however, metaethical
and normative ethical views frequently cluster together,
offering mutual support. Thus it seems no accident that
hedonistic or preference-satisfaction forms of utilitarianism are most often held by metaethical naturalists or that
deontological moral theorists are typically intuitionists or
Kantian constructivists about metaethics. Similarly, the
normative ethical position for which I argue in this chap-

ter can be seen as supporting a rational care theory of welfare, and vice versa.

My normative claim will be that the best life for human beings is one of significant engagement in activities through which we come into appreciative rapport with agent-neutral values, such as aesthetic beauty, knowledge and understanding, and the worth of living beings. An important aspect of a rational care metaethics of welfare is its thesis that welfare's normativity is not agent-relative, but rather agent-neutral, from the perspective of one caring. But if what is good for someone is what it makes sense to want for her for her sake, from the agent-neutral perspective of one caring, then it should not be suprising that whether an activity makes a contribution to her welfare can partly depend on its relation to agent-neutral values. If, therefore, the latter normative claim about human welfare is independently plausible, as I shall argue in this chapter, then that will support, in turn, a rational care metaethics of welfare.

Let us call the proposition that the good life consists of excellent (meritorious or worthy) activity the *Aristotelian Thesis*.[1] I think of a photograph I clipped from the *New York Times* as vividly depicting this claim. It shows a pianist, David Golub, accompanying two vocalists, Victoria Livengood and Erie Mills, at a tribute for Marilyn Horne.[2] All three artists are in fine form, exercising themselves at the height of their powers. The reason I saved the photo, however, is Mr. Golub's face. He is positively grinning, as if saying to himself, "And they *pay* me to do this?"

Mr. Golub's delight is a sign of his activity's value, not what makes it good. His pleasure, in Aristotle's words, "completes the activity . . . as an end which supervenes as the bloom of youth does on those in the flower of their age" (1174b 33–35). The metaphor is apt, since '*eudaimonia*,' Aristotle's term for the human good or welfare, is frequently translated as "flourishing."[3] 'Flourish' comes from the same old French root as 'flower' ('*florir*'). When applied to plants and trees, 'flourish' meant to grow vigorously to the point of putting out leaves or flowers. And a "flourish" was originally the blossom itself.[4] More generally, something flourishes when it thrives or prospers as a healthy plant does coming to full flower. Making the relevant substitutions, Mr. Golub's manifest enjoyment is the sign of his flourishing, its flower or "flourish." What his flourishing consists in, however, is the excellent activity that produces his delight.

In this chapter, I will develop and defend a version of the Aristotelian Thesis that is suggested by the chapter's title. On any interpretation, the Aristotelian Thesis "values activity" in one sense, since it holds that human good derives from certain activities. In addition, I shall argue that these activities themselves involve valuing and the appreciation of value. They are "valuing activities," where the appreciated values differ in kind from the good of a person or value *for* someone. My claim will be that a person's welfare is enhanced, her life is made better *for her*, through active engagement with and appreciation of values whose worth transcends their capacity to benefit (extrinsically or intrinsically). The benefit or contribution to welfare comes through the *appreciative rapport* with the values and the things that have them.

A version of this idea is already implicit in Aristotle. Aristotle says that the virtuous actions in which *eudaimonia* consists are undertaken on account of their distinctive intrinsic value, fineness or nobility (*to kalon*) (1102a5,

1104b 30–1105a 1, 1105a 31, 1115b 12–13,22–24, 1117b 8–10,1119b 16). This already gives us two kinds of value: *eudaimonia*, or welfare, and nobility or fineness of action (*kalon*).[5] Noble activity is what makes up the most beneficial life, but the concept of nobility of action must differ from that of welfare. Otherwise, there could be no substantive disagreement between those who believe that flourishing (welfare) consists of virtuous activity and those who think it resides in something else, such as pleasure or honor. The latter would simply be confused about the concept.

Whereas the concept of welfare is, I have argued, connected to care, nobility of action is conceptually tied to an *ideal* of merit, of what is intrinsically worthy of esteem, emulation, admiration, and praise. To claim as Aristotle does that the most beneficial life involves virtuous activity in his sense, therefore, is already to claim that the best life for a human being involves "valuing activities" in the sense of activities that involve a sense of their own merit.

I believe that Aristotle's proposal has the ring of truth. Human life is shot through with ideal (or, as Charles Taylor calls it, "strong") evaluation in ways that make it inconceivable to me that we can flourish without seeing our lives as expressing ideals we accept.[6] But these are not the only, or even, I think, the most significant, values that are appreciated in a flourishing human life. When I look at the photograph of David Golub, I don't question that he appreciates the merit of his playing, but I doubt that this is the main object of his delight. Rather, I imagine that what his smile primarily reveals is an appreciation of values that *make* music-making a noble pursuit—values like the aesthetic qualities of the music he and his colleagues are making, values that give music importance, significance, or *worth*. And I imagine that the benefit he derives from playing comes, in large measure, through a vivid sense of this worth and his relation to it.

The contrast I have in mind between what I am calling "merit" and "worth" is that between a kind of value (*merit*) that persons and actions have in being worthy of admiration or emulation, on the one hand, and a kind of significance, importance, or "mattering" (*worth*) that something can have by virtue of being appropriately deemed intrinsically significant or important, for example, as an appropriate object of care or (recognition) respect. Both merit and worth are agent-neutral values, presenting themselves as normative for anyone's actions and attitudes. They differ, however, in that what makes actions meritorious, intrinsically worthy of esteem and admiration, is their relation to what has worth.

To see one example of this difference, consider the distinction within Kantian ethics between the kind of value Kant believes a person of good will and her actions have, on the one hand, and, on the other, the value he thinks any person has regardless of whether she has a good will or not. Goodness of will and what Kant calls "moral worth" of actions are forms of *merit*. They are qualities of persons and actions that we credit, praise, admire, encourage, and desire to emulate. The value someone has just by virtue of being a person, on the other hand, is a kind of *worth*, dignity, or "mattering," a value status that makes appropriate certain forms of valuing *conduct* toward the person and certain feelings that are *as of* someone who is to be treated and regarded in those ways.[7] We respond to merit when we admire or are humbled by another's conduct or character. We respond to worth when we see someone as a person who cannot (rightly) be treated in certain ways, who deserves to be treated otherwise.[8]

Nothing in the general ideas of merit and worth ties them specifically to morality, however. The notion of merit can be connected to an ideal of virtually any kind, and merit notions like the noble and the base are prominent in ethical theories, like Aristotle's and Nietzsche's, that are not best viewed as theories of moral right and wrong at all. Nor is there anything in the idea of worth or intrinsic importance that connects it specifically to morality, much less to Kantian ethics. Readers of this essay might agree that philosophy and philosophical activity have intrinsic worth even if they disagree about philosophy's *moral* relevance.

Although they are distinct, I believe that merit and worth are fundamentally related. The relation between them, I think, is that traits or actions are worthy of admiration, they have merit, because they appropriately respond to matters of importance or worth.[9] Thus, parenting is a noble pursuit, it has merit, because it appropriately responds to the importance of children, their significance or worth (as it seems to us they have when we care about them).[10] The creation and appreciation of fine music has merit, because music has worth. And so on. Consequently, my claim will be that we benefit through (meritorious) activities such as parenting and music-making, because these activities involve an appreciation of things that matter, things with worth.

Merit, moreover, is itself a kind of worth, although it cannot be the only kind, since what gives something merit is its responding appropriately to things of worth. Being appropriately related to what has worth matters also. It also has worth. Or, to put the point in more neutral value

terms, being rightly oriented toward intrinsic agent-neutral value is also intrinsically valuable. In what follows, I
shall continue to speak of merit and worth as different
value concepts. However, nothing hangs on this claimed
conceptual difference. We might as easily think of two
kinds of intrinsic agent-neutral value: a basic class (worth)
and a second class (merit) that consists in being properly
oriented to or guided by the first.[11]

The specific version of the Aristotelian Thesis I shall
defend, then, is that the most beneficial human life consists of activities involving the appreciation of worth and
merit. I do not claim that appreciating these values is the
only source of human good. I only claim, somewhat
vaguely, that it is the most important source.

Human Good?

Before I can begin to develop and defend this claim, I
need to make some preliminary distinctions concerning what it could mean to say that human flourishing or
good consists in a life of a certain kind. We can distinguish
four broadly different interpretations of the Aristotelian
Thesis: perfectionist, biological, rational end, and welfare
readings.

PERFECTIONIST INTERPRETATION

According to a perfectionist interpretation, human nature
is intrinsically perfectible.[12] A proper understanding of
what we are includes an understanding of our inherent
potential, of what we should, or are to, become. By ap-
proximating this standard, we better realize our nature,

and hence, ourselves. We get closer to what we ought to be. Departures, on the other hand, are faults or deficiencies, failures to be or achieve what we should. Since development and maturation are also part of our nature, human nature includes not just an ideal blueprint, but also an ideal developmental process.

Perfectionism seems most at home in a metaphysical teleology. The idea of a human *telos* just *is* the idea of an inherently normative human nature. But perfectionism can also simply be asserted as a fundamental normative doctrine, without teleology.[13] This is not, however, the version of the Aristotelian Thesis I shall defend.[14]

BIOLOGICAL INTERPRETATION

The biological interpretation takes its cue from the etymology of 'flourishing' and our conception of what it is for a living being to be in a healthy, prospering condition. This is a familiar enough notion and one with a sufficiently clear application to human beings, no less than to other life forms. No one denies that there is such a thing as human physical health, and talk of psychic or mental health can also be relatively unproblematic.

On the biological interpretation, the Aristotelian Thesis asserts that healthy human functioning consists in virtuous activity. This idea has definite appeal, but I set it aside as well, also without prejudice. Even if the biological interpretation is true, its normative bite depends upon being subsumed under one of the remaining interpretations, the rational end or the welfare interpretation.[15] Only if health is an essential component of human welfare or if, for some other reason, it is a rational human end will the biological interpretation have compelling interest.

RATIONAL END INTERPRETATION

On some readings, what Aristotle means by the "good for man" has nothing necessarily to do with human welfare, but simply with whatever is most finally choiceworthy for human beings.[16] Read this way, the Aristotelian Thesis says that virtuous activity is the single most final and choiceworthy end. Since I will be arguing that merit is grounded in its relation to worth, the rational end interpretation is not one I can accept. Virtuous activity cannot be the most final end if it is made meritorious by responding appropriately to things of worth, since it will then also be pursued for their sake.

WELFARE INTERPRETATION

This leaves the welfare interpretation, according to which the Aristotelian Thesis asserts that a life of virtuous activity is best *for the person herself*, what benefits *her* most. This is the interpretation of the thesis that I will defend.

Although the idea expressed by 'benefit', 'welfare', 'a person's good', 'well-being', and 'prudential value' is common in ethical discussion, a proper analysis and account of its normative status is controversial. Many attempts go wrong, I have argued, because they implicitly make the (Aristotelian) assumption that the agent's good is a highest-level, or most final, rational end that structures all of an agent's first-order rational pursuits. I believe that these accounts go wrong in two ways. They misunderstand the proper scope of welfare, and they mislocate its normative status.[17] As to scope, they mistake whatever a person rationally takes an interest *in*, the set of her rational *interests*, with what is *in her interest* or for her welfare or good. To put it another way, they conflate what is good *from* her point of view with what is good *for* or benefits *her*. I have argued, however, that what benefits a person is not what she rationally wants. It is what anyone, perhaps she herself, would rationally want *for her*, that is, insofar as he or she cared about her.

Thinking about a person's good in this way has implications for its normative status. As I see it, a person's welfare does not exhaust, comprehend, or summarize his rational concerns. Rather, a person has reason to care about his own good because he has reason to care for *himself*. And he has reason to care for himself because he, like any person, has *worth*—he matters. If this is right, rational egoism actually gets things backward. The reason my welfare should matter to me is no different from the reason my welfare should matter to anyone—I am someone who matters (like anyone). Welfare's normativity is not agent-relative; it is agent-neutral.

Nothing in this chapter will depend on a specific metaethical theory of welfare. The Aristotelian Thesis is a proposition of normative ethics, and my claims here are intended, in the first instance, to be metaethically neutral. However, if the Aristotelian Thesis is independently plausible, then this will tend to support a rational care metaethics of welfare for the reasons I have mentioned. And if the rational care theory is independently plausible, that too will support the Aristotelian Thesis.

Ideals and Merit

Merit and demerit are distinctive forms of agent-neutral value and disvalue. Consider the difference, for example, between the intrinsic value of a pleasurable feeling, say, the feeling of a warm shower on a cold day, and that of some meritorious activity, say, a creative endeavor such as writing a play. Both are intrinsically desirable, good things to do in an obvious sense, but only the latter is intrinsically *estimable*. Only the latter can support self-esteem, pride, and other self-evaluations that respond to merit.

What distinguishes merit and demerit as distinctive value forms is their essential connection to distinctive evaluative attitudes—esteem and disesteem, respectively, as these are involved in such emotions and attitudes as admiration, looking up to, being inspired by, desiring to emulate, on the one hand, and contempt, looking down upon, being repelled or repulsed by, desiring to reject, on the other.[18] What has merit is what is *appropriately* an object of such esteem, what it "makes sense" to esteem.[19] And what has demerit is what warrants disesteem.

Consider also the difference between the way in which feeling relates to value in the case of simple pleasures and pains, on the one hand, and in feelings that purport to respond to merit and worth, on the other. Compare the painful feeling of a pin prick with the feeling of shame, say, at being confronted with one's mean-spiritedness. Both feelings are painful, and both have an intrinsic evaluative element. We cannot understand a feeling to be one of pain without seeing it as something bad or something felt as bad. But there is a difference between the ways in which the two feelings involve value (and, as well, between the kinds of value they are felt to involve). Pain presents itself as a *bad feeling*, whereas shame presents itself as a perception of (and response to) a disvalue that has nothing to do with the feeling that reveals it, namely, a shameful (disvaluable) feature in oneself. Of course, since shame is painful, the experience of shame also presents us with an appearance of the badness of the feeling (whether or not the shame is warranted). But what is distinctive about shame is not that it is painful, but that it is a painful appreciation of a disvalue (demerit) that is entirely independent of any disvaluable feeling it might occasion. My shame's object is my shameful mean-spiritedness, demerit in me.

Similarly, pride is not, like the experience of a warm shower on a cold day, simply a pleasurable feeling, but a pleasurable appreciation (except when illusory) of either merit in oneself or reflected merit from someone to whom one is relevantly related. Thus both pride and shame involve the appearance (and, when warranted, the appreciation) of (agent-neutral) values that are distinct from prudential value—merit and demerit, respectively.

Aristotle's terms for what has merit and demerit are 'noble' and 'base'. What is noble are forms of conduct and character that are worthy of us, which we should aspire to and attempt to emulate, and which correspond to an *ideal* of conduct. And what is base is what is beneath us, what we should look down upon and have contempt for, what falls short of the ideal, or perhaps, what corresponds to a "negative ideal."

Aristotle gets to his version of the Aristotelian Thesis via the function argument (1097b 25–1098a 18). The good of everything that has a characteristic function is functioning well. The characteristic function of human beings is activity of soul "implying a rational principle" (1098a 13). So human good must be "activity of soul in conformity with excellence" (1098a 16).

So far this gives us only that human welfare consists in excellent rational activity. What gets us to the conclusion that welfare derives from activity that expresses a *conception* of excellence, specifically, an ideal of the noble, is the distinctive form that, according to Aristotle, human rational functioning takes. Aristotle contrasts merely goal-directed behavior (*poiesis*: producing or making) with the distinctively human activity (*praxis*) that, unlike *poiesis*, aims at an action for its own sake (1140b 6–7). *Praxis* is activity engaged in as intrinsically valuable, as realizing an ideal of action: the noble (*kalon*). So human good must consist in excellent *praxis*, in noble actions chosen on account of their merit.

In addition to the function argument, Aristotle has various dialectical arguments that are addressed to those attracted to other views (1095b 13–1096b 11). An especially persuasive one responds to those who identify *eudaimonia* with honor or esteem. Aristotle agrees that we want esteem, including our own, but he argues that this can't be the root of the matter, since we value the esteem of those *we* esteem more than that of those we hold in low regard. What must explain this, he argues, is that the esteem of the former assures us more of our *worthiness* of esteem, of our merit (1095b 26–29). At bottom, then, we must wish to be virtuous and do what is noble for its own sake.

Aristotle is surely right about the centrality of ideals of merit and demerit in human life. It is obvious that human beings, "the blushing animal," are naturally subject to shame. And we don't need Hobbes, La Rochefoucauld, or evangelical Christianity to persuade us of pride's role in the human psyche. We clearly care about the appearance of merit as well as about actually meriting esteem, as Aristotle's remark about honor shows. How else can we explain the enormous emotional resources we put into defending personal and public narratives in which we come off reasonably well?

As important as merit is to us, however, this doesn't yet explain the specific connection between noble activity and well-being that Aristotle has in mind. So far we just have that noble activity is necessary to something we want to be true—that we have merit. It doesn't follow from this that noble *activity* has intrinsic prudential value. It doesn't follow that a person gets intrinsic benefit from the activity *itself*. The benefit seems to come, rather, from the *fact* of merit or from knowledge or from belief in that fact—as though the benefit of noble activity were that it made the narrative of one's life that of a noble character. As I understand the Aristotelian Thesis, however, the idea is not just that noble activity is necessary to some intrinsically desired fact or state, but that noble activity is *itself* intrinsically valuable for the virtuous person.

Appreciating Value and Worth

To work toward a more adequate understanding of the connection between virtuous activity and prudential value, let us consider a potential (but ultimately misguided) objection to Aristotle's claim that virtuous activity is chosen on account of its merit. Aristotle tells us that to be virtuous, acts must be done as the virtuous person would do them, out of motives that are distinctive of the specific virtue. To manifest the virtue of justice, just acts must be done justly, and to manifest temperance, temperate acts must be done temperately (1105a 30). But Aristotle also says, as we have noted, that virtuous acts must be chosen as noble (1104b 30–1105a 1, 1105a 31, 1117b 8–10). What, then, is the relation between motives of these two different kinds? How can it be the case both that the virtuous person is moved by motives distinctive of the specific virtue she expresses and that she chooses acts on account of their instancing the general feature of nobility?

For example, the courageous person is prepared to face fear and withstand danger when the values at stake warrant doing so. But these values can't themselves include the nobility of the act on pain of circularity. Or to take a non-Aristotelian example, good parenting is virtuous, but the distinctive motive of the good parent would seem to be a concern for one's children, not a desire to exemplify the nobility of good parenting.

The proper response to this objection is to hold that the motives in question need not be incompatible. To be moved by nobility of action in the right way, in the way a virtuous person is, is to be moved by an appreciation of the grounds that *make* the action noble. For example, the courageous person is moved by an appreciation of the values at stake that warrant facing fear and danger and that, therefore, make doing so noble. Facing the danger won't *be* noble unless it is called for by appropriate values (worth), so someone can't be moved by a proper appreciation of an act's nobility unless he is moved also by an appreciation of the values that make the action noble.

There are two distinct points here. One concerns the content of motives expressed in virtuous activity, in particular, that the virtuous person is moved by an awareness of what makes her conduct noble, and not just by the fact of its nobility. The second concerns her motives' distinctive "mode of awareness," specifically, their including an *appreciation* of the relevant values that is not simply a correct belief about their value, but a direct experience and evaluative response to what exemplifies them.

The first point is a consequence of our earlier remarks about the relation between merit and worth. Activity has merit when it is appropriately related to worth. So in order for an activity to be chosen as noble in the right way, it must be chosen for its relation to things of worth, since this is what makes it noble. The importance of children, for instance, calls for giving them good care, so doing so has merit. Parenting is virtuous, therefore, when it expresses an appreciation of the worth of children, the importance of their welfare, and, on those grounds, the merit of good parenting.

Although according to this view an action has merit on account of its relation to worth, there need be nothing consequentialist about this idea. The act is held to be *intrinsically* choiceworthy by virtue of instancing an intrinsically choiceworthy relation to worth. Neither does the fact that merit is derivative from worth entail that meritorious actions must maximize value. That would be so only if the relevant forms of worth were always values to which the appropriate relation is promotion, rather than, say, respect, honoring, or some other such attitude.[20] This is not, I think, the case. For example, meritorious parenting responds to the worth of individual children. The good parent sees his child's welfare as mattering because he sees his *child* as mattering. It is the value of the child that is fundamental, not the value of the state of affairs of his child's faring well.[21] And *the child's* value or worth is not something that can be promoted or produced. It is rather to be respected and cherished. The latter will, of course, involve promoting the child's welfare, but the fundamental reason for doing so will be the child's value.

The second point is that virtuous activity involves a distinctive mode of awareness of merit and worth, namely, *appreciation*, which can differ from belief or other, more abstract, forms of knowledge. The latter are attitudes toward a *proposition* or *fact*, namely, that something has merit or worth (or toward whatever goes proxy for that proposition in the correct noncognitivist account, if there is one).[22] The former, however, involves feelings, experiences, and attitudes toward the meritorious or worthy thing *itself*. It is impossible to be in the state of directly experiencing or appreciating someone's merits, for example, without esteeming *her* and her traits, although this is possible when one simply believes or knows *that* she has these merits. Similarly, it is impossible to directly appreciate something's worth without being in the state of deeming or holding *it* important, without its seeming to one as if it matters. In this way appreciation is a quasi-perceptual state. It involves experiences *of* merit and worth, where this involves an experienced valuing relation to a particular thing.[23]

Return now to the criticism that if a person chooses to act on account of an act's nobility, then he will not be moved as a virtuous person would. In effect, the objection assumes that Aristotle holds that the virtuous person is moved by a *de dicto* desire to act nobly, a desire that it be true that he does the noble thing, whatever that might be.[24] And the objection is that if that is so, then the person's motives will not have the appropriate relation to the specific things of worth with which the situation confronts him. We can begin to respond to this objection, we noted, if we say that a virtuous person will not simply act out of the conviction that a given act is noble, but, as well, out of convictions concerning the source of its merit in values (things of worth) to which the act responds. Thus, the good parent takes pains for his children in the belief that so acting is noble because it responds in the appropriate way to his children's worth.

If we go only so far, however, a version of the objection can be raised again at this stage. If I act simply in the *belief* that children have worth, mine included, without directly *appreciating* my children's worth, without some direct sense or experience of this value *in them* (for example, through sympathetic concern), then the attitudes I express in parenting will be neither toward my parenting activity nor toward my children, whose importance I take to warrant it. It will rather be toward the propositions that they have worth and that, because they do, my parenting activity has merit.

That this is not what Aristotle has in mind is shown by his distinction between virtue and continence (1145a 15–1152a 32).[25] Unlike the merely continent, the virtuous person chooses noble acts "for *their* own sakes," in the sense that her favorable regard is directed to the acts themselves, not to propositions or states of affairs that include them (1105a 30–32, emphasis added). The virtuous have an intrinsic regard for their activity which turns into enjoyment when they engage in it. They take wholehearted pleasure in the activity itself. Ross's translation has Aristotle saying that the temperate person doesn't simply abstain from bodily pleasures, but "delights in this very fact" (1104b 6). But clearly what Aristotle means is not that she delights in the (contemplated) fact of her temperance, but that she delights in temperate *activity*. She may also delight in contemplating the fact of her temperance, but that isn't what makes her temperate. Irwin's translation expresses the point better: "if someone who abstains from bodily pleasures enjoys the abstinence itself, then he is temperate."[26] Temperance is revealed in the temperate person's undivided engagement with and enjoyment of his temperate activity. His "activity is intensified by *its* proper pleasure" (1175a 30, emphasis added).

There is a sense in which both the continent person and the virtuous person choose noble activities for their own sake, since both act in the conviction that their actions are intrinsically worth choosing. But there is another sense in which only the virtuous person chooses noble acts for *their* own sake, since only she acts out of a directly appreciative regard for the activity itself *de re* (and, if I am right, out of a regard for specific things of worth that give them merit). If we identify desires by that-clauses, then both the virtuous and the continent act out of the same desire, that they act nobly. A consequence of what we have just been saying, however, is that this identity obscures an important difference in the *ways* that the continent and the virtuous respectively desire to do what is noble for its own sake.

This points to a more general distinction between ways in which someone may desire to do something for its own sake. Someone may think an activity intrinsically desirable and act out of a desire that she engage in it without having any favorable regard for the activity itself of a sort that would naturally become enjoyment were it to turn out as she envisages it. Having the belief, she may just want the narrative of her life to include the performance of that activity. If, contrary to fact, she could make it true that she had engaged in the activity without having actually to engage in it, she might be indifferent or even pleased. Consider the difference, for example, between an enthusiastic music-lover and someone who, lacking any experienced appreciation and enthusiasm for the activity, nonetheless engages in musical activity because she believes it an intrinsically desirable thing to do. The first person takes pleasure in musical activity, whereas any pleasure taken by the second is in contemplating, self-reflectively, the fact that she engages in it.[27] The second acts out of a *de dicto* desire to make it true that she engage in meritorious musical activity. The first acts out of a *de re* desire for musical activity that, since it is directed at the activity itself, becomes enjoyment when its object is realized.

Unlike merely continent actions, therefore, virtuous activity is actively enjoyed. The virtuous person favorably regards what he is doing *de re*, not just, *de dicto*, the fact that he is doing it. However, he also acts on account of his activity's merit. So his enjoyment cannot simply be like that one has in taking a warm shower on a cold day. It must be a pleasurable appreciation, not just of a quality of his own feeling, but of the value (merit) of his activity. It must involve an appearance that is as of his activity's merit, which appearance is itself properly related to warrant for his esteem.[28]

The lesson of our first point, however, is that it cannot involve only this. To choose an action on account of its nobility in the right way is to choose it out of a regard for its orientation to things of worth and, consequently, out of a regard for those very values. It follows that the proper enjoyment of virtuous activity involves an appreciation of these latter values also—appearances that are as of things of worth, which appearances are related appropriately to warrant for seeing things in that way.

There are two components, then, to a proper answer to the objection that virtuous activity involves motives characteristic of specific virtues rather than the desire to do what is noble. The first is that virtuous activity does, indeed, involve an appropriate relation to merit-making worth. And the second is that this relation includes an intrinsically motivating appreciation of the activity's orientation to things that matter.

The Benefit of Merit- and Worth-Appreciating Activity

A friend once told me that she was unprepared for what a profoundly moving experience parenting would be for her. What she meant, I think, is that through parenting she was brought into a direct appreciation of deeply important values—the worth of her children, the importance their being raised well, and, consequently, the value of the activity in which she was herself engaged.[29] The activity itself included experiences and feelings that were *as of* her children's value and the value of parenting them well. Neither of us was in any doubt, moreover, about whether she meant also to be saying something about the contribution this activity was making to her own well-being, the value of her own life for her. She was saying that parenting had enriched her life, that she had found a depth of satisfaction in it for which she had not really been prepared.

I think I see a similar sense in David Golub's face. He may be having more fun than parenting can sometimes seem to involve, but any deeply worthwhile activity re-

quires serious and painstaking attention, and no doubt
there are days when practicing a demanding piece seems
anything but fun. What is common to both activities is
the experience of connecting with something of worth in
a way that enables the direct appreciation of the value of
one's activity.

Both activities give pleasure, but, as Aristotle says, pleasure is a sign of the activities' value, not its substance.
What is pleasurable is, at least partly, the appreciation of
merit and worth that these activities themselves involve.
And what makes these pleasures loom so large in our welfare is the sense that, through them, we are connecting
with things that matter. The benefit comes through the
appreciation of agent-neutral values—worth and merit—
with which these activities connect us.

The same is true, I believe, with the more canonical
Aristotelian virtues—courage, temperance, justice, and so
on. What is so satisfying about meeting challenges with
courage, for example? Is it the mere fact of overcoming
fear or inconfidence? No doubt this is part of it, but surely
it is largely the sense of having dealt with these obstacles
when and because it *mattered*, when, that is, the values at
stake called for doing so. We won't count an act as one of
bravery, or, at least, credit it as such, unless we can see it
as an appropriate response to things of worth.

That the primary source of prudential value is a felt
appreciation of valuable activity, and not just belief or
knowledge, can be seen by considering how these respectively relate to self-esteem. It is possible to believe that
one deserves esteem, including one's own, but nonetheless to lack self-esteem. Self-esteem is an attitude and disposition to certain feelings toward oneself, not just an

evaluative belief about oneself. It is a way of regarding oneself that includes a sense or feelings as of one's own value or a disposition to such feelings.[30] One can be racked by feelings of inadequacy and so lack self-esteem even as one believes that one shouldn't.[31] Although one judges there is no warrant for feeling this way, one may be unable to shake feelings that are as of one's inadequacies. It seems clear that a person is substantially worse off by virtue of regarding herself in this way and not just because of the undesirability of her feelings as feelings. Although she believes she has merit, she is deprived of a stable appreciation of her merit. She does not experience herself as having worth or merit. From the standpoint from which she normally lives her life, it is as if she has little or no merit, as if her activity does not connect in the right way with what has real significance and worth.

How do we gain the appreciation of merit in which self-esteem consists? If merit consists in responding appropriately to worth, then we can sense our merit only through sensing our responding appropriately to worth. This is just what we gain in activities of merit, since they are guided by an appreciation of worth. Of course, as Aristotle's remark about honor reminds us, being honored by those we honor can support self-esteem also. But it cannot do so simply by confirming the belief that we have merit, since we can have that belief and lack self-esteem. It must rather support a sense or felt appreciation of our merit, and this requires that others have this sense, which we can then receive from them empathetically, seeing ourselves through their eyes. For that to be true, however, they must be able to sense or see merit in us by appreciating our virtuous activity.

If this is right, then the good of virtuous activity derives primarily from a quasi-perceptual, felt relation between the person and merit-making values that such activity usually involves. Both the subjective and objective elements are necessary. If what a person experiences as having merit and worth doesn't have it in fact, then her life has less value (including prudential value) than she supposes. To check this, consider what kind of life you would want for someone you care about, for that person's own sake. Will it be a matter of indifference to you whether what the person herself takes to ground her activities' merit really has worth or not? If you are convinced that what she is devoting herself to is worthless, would you want this for her for her sake as much as you would if the thing she were devoted to were something you thought had worth? It seems obvious to me that I would not. By the same token, however, neither is it a matter of indifference whether a person whose activities actually have merit are felt by her to do so. The really significant benefits of virtuous activity require both subjective and objective elements. Related in the right way, these constitute an appreciation of the activity's merit and relation to worth, namely, an appearance as of its merit and relation to worth, which appearance is itself appropriately related to actual merit and worth.

I am not claiming that illusory satisfactions have no value for the person, nor that really meritorious, but unappreciated, activities are without benefit. My claim is simply that virtuous activity that includes an experience or appreciation of its relation to worth has far greater value for the person than either the subjective or the objective element, taken by itself.[32]

Virtuous Activity and Relationship

To this point, I have been discussing individuals' virtuous activities more or less independently of their relations to others. I have been supposing, of course, that many virtuous activities, like parenting, derive merit from forms of relationship to others. But I have been abstracting from ways in which others are involved in virtually every form of valuable activity, ways in which shared valuable activities make possible distinctively valuable forms of relationship, and ways in which acknowledging the values that ground merit can lead one to acknowledge the value of persons.

The basic idea underlying many of these points is simple enough. Unlike welfare, merit and worth are not value *for* anyone. Something enhances welfare by being good *for someone*, but there is no such thing as merit or worth for someone, except in the sense of someone thinking something has merit or worth. There is only merit or worth period.

Consequently, if worth or merit is normative for distinctive evaluative attitudes, they must be normative for such attitudes in *anyone*, normative for such attitudes *as from anyone's perspective*. When we see something as worthy of admiration and emulation, we see it as having a feature, merit, that is there for anyone to appreciate who is capable of doing so. Similarly, if I see something, like fine music, to have worth, then I take it to be something anyone would be warranted in deeming important.

Because they are not appreciated or regarded from any *particular* standpoint, merit and worth can be *common* values—they and their appreciation can be shared. Moreover, appreciating these values through shared valuable activity makes possible distinctive forms of valuable relationship, through which the agent-neutral value of these activities is both confirmed and ramified. This, in turn, creates new forms of shared valuable activity that both adds prudential value of its own and supports that of the initial activities.

Merit ramifies both "up" and "out." It ramifies up, because when something has merit, then so do various second- and higher-order attitudes toward that thing. And it ramifies out, because when something has merit, then so also do various attitudes of others toward it. The explanation for both phenomena derives from the nature of merit, its consisting in an appropriate response to worth.

For example, since individual persons have worth, and since various forms of love and respect are appropriate responses to their worth, these have merit. The appropriate response to merit is the esteem of admiration and the desire to emulate. Because these are appropriate responses to merit, then they are also appropriate responses, at one remove, to worth. So they have merit also. Or alternatively, because merit is a form of worth, to which they respond appropriately, this gives them merit also. And this can ramify up again. Since esteem for merit has merit, then esteem for esteem for merit has merit also. And so on.

Merit ramifies out, because if something has merit, then it calls for esteem from others no less than from the person who has it. Since merit consists in the appropriate response to worth, and esteem is the appropriate response to merit, then esteem is the appropriate response, at one remove, to worth. So others' esteem of our merit has merit also. (Or, alternatively, this is so because merit is a form of worth to which others' esteem is the appropriate response.) And this can ramify out again. So esteem for a person's esteem for another person's merit has merit also. And so on.

Merit's ramifying upward and outward creates a rich structure for the shared appreciation of valuable activity. And, as I have argued, the appreciation of her relation to worth is a major source of prudential value for a virtuous person, merit's ramifying up and out creates a rich set of possibilities for the appreciation of value to enhance welfare. When two people share esteem for merit, whatever its source, they are then in a position to appreciate this meritorious response in each other, and then, to appreciate the merit of their so doing, and so on. And when the merit they appreciate is in each other, these effects are accentuated. Moreover, since, as Joseph Brodsky put it, "a man is what he loves," in esteeming another's valuings one also appreciates and esteems that person as well.[33]

An unusual example will help illustrate these points. Oliver Sacks describes the remarkable case of twins who had been variously diagnosed as autistic, psychotic, or severely retarded and institutionalized since the age of seven.[34] When Sacks first got to know the twins, they were twenty-six years old and considered to be relatively uninteresting *idiot savant* calculators, whose "trick" was that they were able instantly to calculate the day of the week of any date within the past, or the next, 40,000 years. It was thought that they did this by mechanically applying an algorithm. The more Sacks got to know them, however, the clearer it became to him that the twins actually had a remarkable intuitive feel for mathematical structure

and a rich shared imaginative life contemplating its
beauty together.

> They were seated in a corner together, with a mysterious
> "secret" smile on their faces, a smile I had never seen be-
> fore, enjoying the strange pleasure and peace they now
> seemed to have. I crept up quietly, so as not to disturb
> them. They seemed to be locked in a singular, purely nu-
> merical converse. John would say a number—a six-figure
> number. Michael would catch the number, nod, smile, and
> seem to savor it. Then he in turn would say another six-
> figure number, and it was John who received, and appreci-
> ated it richly. . . . *What* were they doing? What on earth
> was going on?[35]

Sacks finally conjectured that what was happening was
that John and Michael were exchanging gifts of very
large prime numbers. Somehow each was able to see
the primeness of a six-digit number and propose it as an
object of shared contemplation. To test his hypothesis,
Sacks returned to the ward with a book of primes. Finding the twins, "closeted in their numerical communion,"
he writes,

> I decided to join in, and ventured an eight-figure prime.
> They both turned toward me, then suddenly became still,
> with a look of intense concentration, and perhaps wonder
> on their faces. There was a long pause—the longest I had
> ever known them to make, it must have lasted a half-min-
> ute or more—and then suddenly, simultaneously, they
> both broke into smiles.[36]

This "great joy," Sacks remarks, was actually a "double
joy." Sacks had introduced John and Michael to a new and
remarkably large prime they had never before encoun-

tered, and he had made it evident to them that he had understood what they were up to, "admired it," and wanted to join in the activity himself. At this point, the twins made a place for Sacks, and the group continued on, now a prime-contemplating threesome, with Sacks sneaking looks at his book to confirm what John and Michael could see with mathematical intuition.

Sacks's account recalls G. E. Moore's remark that "by far the most valuable things, which we know or can imagine," are "the pleasures of human intercourse and the enjoyment of beautiful objects."[37] Moore was speaking, not of a person's good, but of what he called "good absolutely."[38] However, his remark has something approaching the ring of truth when we interpret in relation to welfare. What explains this, I think, is the interpretation of the Aristotelian Thesis I have been offering, namely, that the prudential value of virtuous activity consists largely in the appreciation of its connection to worth. Beauty is a form of worth, the appropriate responses to which include creation and appreciation. So both creating and appreciating beauty have merit, and these activities can enrich lives because they involve the pleasurable appreciation of this merit and worth. Similarly, the pleasures of human intercourse largely consist, I believe, in appreciating the merits and worth of other persons as well as the merit of relating to them in various ways.

Because merit ramifies up and out, its appreciation ramifies up and out also. This means that the prudential value of an individual instance is likely to be substantially enhanced and supported by the prudential value of its branching offshoots. In this way, virtuous activity tends to create and partake of coherent structures of mutually supporting prudential value.

Conclusion

Nothing I have said in support of the Aristotelian Thesis has presupposed any particular metaethics of well-being. Nonetheless, I believe that the rational care theory of welfare I presented in Chapters I and II and the arguments I have provided for the Aristotelian Thesis in this chapter are mutually supporting. When I ask myself what kind of life it makes sense to want for my children, it just seems obvious to me that it is a life in which they engage in activities whose merit and relation to worth they themselves appreciate. I would like it just fine if they came to have the same smile that I see on David Golub's face (or that Oliver Sacks saw on John's and Michael's faces).

Moreover, as I mentioned before in Chapter I, a rational care theory tends to support the Aristotelian Thesis in another way. According to a rational care account, we make assessments of welfare, not from the (agent-relative) perspective of the person whose welfare is in question, but from the (agent-neutral) perspective of someone who cares for her. It therefore should not be surprising that evaluations of welfare are sensitive to judgments of the agent-neutral values of merit and worth in the way the Aristotelian Thesis claims.

The Aristotelian Thesis is plausible independently of any particular metaethics of a person's good. Because it is, it provides some support for the particular metaethics I have suggested, since that theory itself supports the Aristotelian Thesis.

Of course, this support might not seem very significant, since it might be thought that something's being good for someone is what makes it make sense to want it for them for their sake, and not vice versa. But we have the arguments of Chapter I that tell against that possibility. If being good for someone were a concept that is independent of the concept of being something we should want for someone for her sake, then either the concept of welfare would not itself be a normative concept, or it would have to have some normativity other than for sympathetic concern. If we accept the former, then we will need some further premise to convince us why the fact that something is good for someone should be of concern from *any* perspective, the agent's own or any other. And the most widely held version of the latter, that welfare has an agent-relative normativity, should at this point seem both implausible and to make it a mystery why the fact that something is good agent-neutrally should bear on what it would make sense to want *for someone* for her own sake. Once we remove these two remaining possibilities, the Aristotelian Thesis can be seen to lend its plausibility to a rational care theory of welfare.

Notes

Chapter I: *Welfare's Normativity*

1. This is also sometimes referred to as "prudential value." See, for example, Griffin 1986 and Sumner 1996, 20–21.

2. I am indebted to Elizabeth Anderson for the point that caring involves valuing the individual person, rather than a state involving her, and to David Velleman for this term in this context. See Anderson 1993, 26–30. I am also indebted throughout this book to feminist approaches to ethical philosophy, some inspired by Gilligan 1982, that have stressed the importance of care. To list only a few: Baier 1994, Blum 1980, and Noddings 1984.

3. Mill 1979, Ch. IV, §6–7.

4. Different kinds of empathy and sympathy are discussed in Chapter III.

5. On this point, see Overvold 1980.

6. Kant 1997, 28, Ak. 417.

7. Greenspan 1975; Hare 1971, 81–127; Darwall 1983, 15–17, 43–50; Korsgaard 1997; Broome 1999.

8. I discuss this further in Darwall 2001, and in relation to Hobbes's thought in Darwall 2000.

9. It might be objected that it is impossible to care about someone and not be guided by his good (at least as one sees it). If so, it would be false that one who cares *ought* to be guided by the good of the cared for, since it would be impossible for her not to be. The same objection might be raised to the relation

between ends and means. It might be said that it is impossible for someone really to have something as an end and fail to take what he believes to be necessary means. And if that were so, the principle of instrumental rationality would not be normative but descriptive. However, means/end irrationality is indeed possible, perhaps even frequent. Christine Korsgaard gives the case of a wounded Western movie character, Tex, who aims to live but struggles against the doctor's attempt to saw off his gangrenous leg, even as he acknowledges it is his only hope to stay alive (Korsgaard 1997, 238; see also Korsgaard 1986, 13–14). Similarly, we can imagine someone who cares for Tex acknowledging that he won't live without this extreme measure, but, perhaps because of an empathic response to the more proximate threat of the pain, helps Tex in his struggle against the doctor. In such case, we will want to say that, much as it will be painful, it will be better for Tex to undergo the amputation, and, insofar as he cares about Tex, he ought to aid, not obstruct, this process.

10. One is committed to this hypothesis, not in the sense that to care about it *is* to accept or believe it, but that in caring it will *seem* to one that the other is worth caring for and that one's caring will itself be justified only if the cared for is worth caring for. Similar points hold with having something as end. One can have ends that one doesn't believe are worth having, but in having an end it will seem to one as if the end is something to be brought about, and having the end will make sense, will be warranted, only if this is the case.

11. For a related idea, see Velleman 1999.

12. What we have said so far should already make us doubt that concern for someone can be understood in terms of a sensitivity to his welfare. The object of care is no fact or state, but the person himself, and, as we have seen, desires may track a person's welfare without involving any concern for the person.

13. I am indebted in what follows to Velleman 1996.

14. Hume 1978, 415, 458. Further references will be placed in the text: (T.).

15. I borrow these terms from Velleman.

16. That is, they cannot coherently disagree about whether there is epistemic reason to believe p. They might, of course, disagree about whether there are pragmatic reasons to be in the state of believing p.

17. Or, also equivalently, whether, insofar as they care about S, they ought to desire X for S.

18. On the model of "good-" or "value-making" properties more generally. Thus hedonism is generally understood as holding, not just that the class of intrinsically prudentially valuable things is restricted to pleasurable experiences, but that what *makes* an experience prudentially valuable is that it is pleasurable. Both of these claims, however, differ from the metaethical claim about what welfare itself is or what the concept of welfare involves.

19. Since, for example, an intrinsic desire for another's good might arise simply through psychological association. See pp. 1–2 above.

20. This seems to be the sense that Harry Frankfurt has in mind in Frankfurt 1988.

21. The sense of respect I have in mind here is "recognition respect" rather than "appraisal respect." Respecting someone (as a person) in the recognition sense is a matter of regulating one's conduct with respect to him in whatever ways are required by his being a person (say, respecting his autonomy as a free and equal rational agent). Respecting someone in the appraisal sense, on the other hand, involves an appraisal or evaluation of a person's conduct and character. For this distinction, seeDarwall 1977. The claims in the text exclusively concern recognition respect for someone as a person.

22. On the distinction between agent-relative (or agent-centered) and agent-neutral reasons, see Nagel 1970 and 1986 (164–188); Scheffler 1982; and Parfit, 1984.

23. I take this useful term from Noddings 1984.

24. On this point, see Darwall 1995, 207–237. According to Joachim Hruschka, the first formulation of the utility principle was due to Leibniz. See Hruschka 1991.

25. Bentham, oddly enough, is a more complex figure in these terms. Although it is little noted, the argument that Bentham gives for the principle of utility in *The Principles of Morals and Legislation* is actually respect-based, since he claims that it is uniquely suited to provide a principle for noncoercive public moral discussion. The idea is that because whether something promotes utility can be ascertained by empirical methods, irrespective of the moral opinions of the inquirers, arguments made on its basis do not inherently presume that others already share one's moral opinions. For an analysis of Bentham's argument along these lines, see Darwall 1994.

26. For an introduction to the subject that treats the great ethical philosophers (Aristotle, Hobbes, Kant, Mill, and Nietzsche) as philosophical ethicists, in this sense, see Darwall 1998.

27. I have been helped here by discussion with Katie McShane.

Chapter II: *Welfare and Care*

1. Not to worry: Tarzan and Jane are happily reunited at the end of the novel.

2. On this point, see Overvold 1980.

3. An attitude is said to be *de se* if it includes an ineliminable reference to himself or herself (the bearer of the attitude), as in: "He believes *he* is always being persecuted." See Lewis 1979.

4. Here is another poignant example. As I write in December 2001, Iran's theocratic hierarchy is cracking down on citizens who seek democratic reform. The remark of a relative of one of the imprisoned dissidents is telling: "They could have had much better lives than they had. The suffering they are

experiencing right now is the price they are paying for reform" ("Iran Intensifies Crackdown on Opposition," *New York Times*, December 8, 2001).

5. This distinction is sometimes put as that between prudential value and perfectionist value. On the distinction between prudential and perfectionist value, see Sumner 1995.

6. Sidgwick 1967, 111–112. (Further references will be noted in the text as ME.) Richard Brandt offered a similar definition of welfare in Brandt 1972, 686. John Rawls relies on Sidgwick's formulation in defining a rational life plan for a person in Rawls 1971, 408. Peter Railton offers an account of a person's good in Sidgwick's manner, but with an important revision. For Railton, what is for a person's good is not what that person would want if he were fully informed, but what a fully informed version of himself would want for himself as he actually is (Railton 1986a). This avoids what Robert K. Shope called the "conditional fallacy" (see Shope, 1978a and 1978b). Railton, however, distinguishes between a person's good and her welfare. See note 21 below. James Griffin also defends a kind of informed-desire account in Griffin 1986. In *Impartial Reason*, I followed Sidgwick's formulation as an account of a rational conception of the good life, but distinguished it from an account of the person's good for reasons I hope to clarify and develop here. See Darwall 1983, 105.

For criticisms of full-information accounts of a person's good, see Velleman 1988; Sobel 1994; and Rosati 1995.

7. Griffin 1977.

8. This kind of example tells also against John Skorupski's view that, although there are things a person has reason to do that are not part of his welfare, welfare nonetheless consists in what a person has reason to desire. It seems reasonable to attribute to Tarzan a reasonable desire that Jane be happy and so remain with Clayton and not just think that he has reason to promote her happiness. See Skorupski 1999, 119–133.

9. Parfit 1984, 494.

10. See the references to Robert K. Shope and Peter Railton in note 6.

11. Overvold 1980, 117n-118n. Overvold formulates this restriction to deal with a "self-sacrifice" objection to the informed-desire account of self-interest that Richard Brandt proposes in Brandt 1972.

12. Kavka 1986, 41.

13. In fairness to Kavka, we should note that his primary interest is to fashion a category of "self-interested desire" for a workable formulation of psychological egoism, in order to evaluate whether Hobbes was a psychological egoist. A conception of self-interested desires broader than desires for self-interest might well be preferable for that purpose.

14. So what makes a motive selfish? Good question. If selfishness is not always an (excessive) form of self-concern, it must include other forms of self-obsession (arrogance, for example) as well.

15. This does not entail that things outside the boundaries of a life cannot be part of something that does make an intrinsic difference to the person's welfare. Being a good parent and giving my children upbringings suitable to their futures may be an important constituent of my welfare—it may be part of what I want for *my* sake as well as for theirs—and its success conditions will depend on occurrences beyond my life's boundaries. On this point, see Parfit 1984, 495.

16. Parfit 1984, 494.

17. The success theory should also be understood to include a restriction to intrinsic desires. To see this, consider Tarzan's situation. Tarzan desires (informedly, we may suppose) that Jane be happy, but the satisfaction of this desire does not advance his interest according to the success theory since its object (Jane's happiness) is not itself part of his life. To use Overvold's formulation, it is not a logically necessary condition of Jane's being happy that Tarzan exist. But consider Tarzan's (derived) desire that he live the rest of his life without Jane. This *is* a desire that satisfies Overvold's restriction. Suppose that Tar-

zan's view of things is correct, that Jane really would be happier if he were never to see her again. It will then be true that this is what Tarzan would want most with full information and experience. But if the satisfaction of his desire for Jane's happiness is not in his interest, then the satisfaction of his desire to live the rest of his life without her can hardly be so if the only reason he has the latter desire is because he has the former.

18. I do not, of course, mean that if my concern for someone makes me want something for her that this is sufficient for that thing to be something that would actually be good for her. It must be something it makes sense for someone who cares about her to want for her for her own sake.

19. For the distinction between "now for then" and "then for then" preferences, see Hare 1981, 101–106.

20. Williams 1981.

21. Something like this may be at work in Peter Railton's remark that his distinctive informed-desire account of a person's good should not be regarded as an account of that person's "welfare." See Railton 1986b, 30 (footnote 10).

22. Of course, some may, like the pleasure of knowing that I will be going. I take it for granted that it is the (enduring) person who benefits, not a "person-stage." On this point, see Brink 1992.

23. For someone or other. See Sidgwick 1967, Bk. III, Ch. XIV, "Ultimate Good." I'm not sure if this is precisely what Derek Parfit has in mind when he cites the "in harmony with reason" formulation to show that Sidgwick holds what he (Parfit) calls a "critical present-aim theory," but it supports that conclusion. See Parfit 1984, 500.

24. Sidgwick 1884, 108, emphasis added. This passage is quoted and usefully discussed in Crisp 1990.

25. Of course, Sidgwick doesn't really think that reason dictates that we care about ourselves or others in the sense I have in mind either. Rather, he thinks that among the self-evident axioms are rational dictates such as "a smaller present good is not to be preferred to a greater future good," "a rational being

is bound to aim at good generally, . . . not merely a particular part of it," and so on (ME.381, 382). However, to arrive at the principles of rational prudence and benevolence, these must themselves be interpreted in terms (indeed, solely in terms) of persons' goods, of what is good *for persons*. That is, it must be true that what is good for persons (either for oneself or for personal generally) should matter to a rational agent. And I can't see how that could be true unless practical reason could somehow dictate that one care for oneself (and for others).

I should also stress that in saying that rational agency doesn't itself include the capacity to care for someone for his own sake (to have what I shall be calling "sympathetic concern"), I don't mean to foreclose the Kantian possibility that it does include some form of valuing individuals for their sake, namely, (recognition) respect. On this, see pp. 14–16 above.

26. It is consistent with this that there could be a derivative rational requirement for agents with a certain kind of psychology (maybe ours) to care, if rational deliberation would give rise, given their psychology, to concern.

27. See the discussion of this point in Chapter I, pp. 7–8.

28. Compare, for example, Williams 1981 with Korsgaard 1986. The term "internalism requirement" derives from Korsgaard's article. I discuss the intuitive ideas underlying empirical naturalist internalism, on the one hand, and autonomist internalism, on the other, in Darwall 1992. I discuss the development of these two traditions among the seventeenth- and eighteenth-century British Moralists in Darwall 1995.

29. Parfit 1984, 117–194.

30. See note 23.

31. Korsgaard construes the internalism requirement in this broad way in Korsgaard 1986.

32. Note that internalists are by no means restricted to anything like Brandtian cognitive psychotherapy as a deliberative ideal. I argue for a more Kantian ideal in Darwall 1983, 201–239.

33. Parfit 1984, 141–142.

34. As David Brink has argued in Brink 1992.

35. On this point, see Brink 1992.

36. One strategy, which might make clear both your concern and your respect for Sheila, would be to offer to care for her during her illness. This would communicate to her the seriousness of your estimate of the costs she is imposing on herself (and on people who care about her) as well as your respect. I thank Jennifer Roback Morse for this suggestion.

37. See above, pp. 10–11.

38. That is, a normative claim that is intrinsic to the concept of welfare. It may follow from a theory of rationality together with facts about an agent's psychological makeup that rational deliberation (including, say, vivid consideration of a person's plight) would trigger psychological mechanisms leading that agent to care. And if that were so, then a person's interest would have a normative claim on such an agent. Maybe each of us is such an agent.

39. See pp. 1–2 above.

40. On this point, see Anderson 1993, 26–30.

Chapter III: *Empathy, Sympathy, Care*

1. Eisenberg 1991. See also Eisenberg and Strayer 1987, especially 3–13. Compare Martin Hoffman's definition: "empathic distress is defined as a feeling that is more appropriate to the suffering person's condition than to the observer's own relatively comfortable circumstances" (Hoffman 1991, 132). See also Hoffman 1978.

2. This point is emphasized in Stocker and Hegeman 1996, 214–217.

3. I discuss certain key aspects of Smith's views in the context of a review of recent literature on Smith in Darwall 1999. For an excellent discussion of Smith in general, see Griswold 1999.

4. Titchener 1909; Lipps 1903 and 1905; see Wispé 1991, 78, and Davis 1996, 5.

5. See also Scanlon 1998, 108–143.

6. See note 6 in Chapter II.

7. I am defending here a claim I first made in Darwall 1983, 160–163.

8. Carl Rogers distinguishes between the "internal frame of reference" of empathy and the "external frame of reference" of sympathy. See Rogers 1951.

Of course, although empathy and concern differ in this way, one way of showing concern (sympathy) for someone can be to empathize with her.

9. Scheler 1954, 14–18. See also Wispé 1991, 76–77.

10. Hume also quotes Horace in this connection, "the human countenance . . . borrows smiles or tears from the human countenance." Hume 1975, 220. Further references will be noted thus in the text: (E.).

11. This statement must be modified to take account of the problem of the general point of view, which Hume claims in the *Treatise* we solve by projecting into the perspective of those who interact with the person whose merit we are trying to judge (T.581–583). However, the problem to which this solution responds is itself created by a variety of sympathy, that is, contagion, that involves no projection. Hume calls the distinctive, moral-sentiment-involving species of sympathy, "extensive sympathy" (T.586). For a discussion of this difference, see Abramson 1997.

12. Meltzoff and Moore 1977 and 1983. See also Bavelas et al., 1987, 319, 334.

13. Darwin 1872.

14. Ekman 1985. For further discussion, see Frank 1988, 113–114.

15. Ekman 1992; Ekman and Davidson 1993. These studies are discussed further in Damasio 1994, 148–149.

16. For a general review, see Adelman and Zajonc 1989. See also Zajonc, Murphy, and Inglehart 1989.

17. Simner 1971.

18. Hoffman 1987, 51. See also Hoffman 1984.

19. Bavelas et al., 1987, 323.

20. Bavelas, Lemery, and Mullet 1986.

21. As described in Bavelas et al., 1987, 329–330.

22. Linnert 1982. Cited by Thompson 1987, and discussed by Goldman 1993, 353.

23. Butterworth and Cochran 1980; Butterworth 1991.

24. Smith 1976, 9. Further references will be placed in the text: (TMS.).

25. Gordon 1986, 1992, and 1995; Goldman 1989, 1992.

26. Kahneman and Tversky 1982.

27. Striking evidence for simulation comes also from developmental studies and, most impressively, from studies of autistic children. In an experiment by Baron-Cohen and colleagues, which Goldman cites, children witnessed a scene in which a doll protagonist sees a marble placed in a particular location. Then, when the doll is off scene, the marble's location is switched. When the doll returns, the children were asked where the doll believes the marble is. Eighty-five percent of nonautistic children answered correctly, while only 20 percent of autistic children did. The other 80 percent of the autistic children could not distinguish between where *they* believed the marble was and where the doll did. Moreover, this deficiency cannot be explained as lacking some aspect of general intelligence, since 86 percent of a pool of Down's syndrome children answered correctly. Goldman argues that the explaining factor probably has to do with the extreme poverty of pretend play associated with autism. Because they are worse at simulating the doll by imaginative pretense, they are worse at attributing beliefs to it. (See Baron-Cohen, Leslie, and Frith 1985.)

28. On this point, see, for example, Roberts 1988 and Greenspan 1981.

29. The need for "unself-consciously" will be apparent in the next section.

30. Strawson 1968.

31. On the importance of normative discussion about how to feel, see Gibbard 1990, especially 73–80.

32. Stotland 1969. For a general review, see Davis 1996, 114–115.

33. Hoffman 1981. See also Hoffman 1991.

34. Batson and Shaw 1991, 113. See also Batson 1991.

35. This research is most fully described in Batson 1991.

36. Baston 1991, 5–6.

37. Again, I am indebted here to Elizabeth Anderson's work and to David Velleman.

38. Or, as I suggested in Chapter I, we might imagine such an intrinsic desire arising as a result of the kind of conditioning by which Mill explains (in *Utilitarianism*) the genesis of an intrinsic desire for wealth.

39. While we can't simply take these appearances at face value, I believe we can nonetheless vindicate their justificatory force within a general theory of practical reasons. For an attempt, see Darwall 1983, especially Part III.

CHAPTER IV: *Valuing Activity: Golub's Smile*

1. Aristotle 1980. Aristotle's translators prefer 'virtuous'. We should bear in mind, however, that the excellences of character that Aristotle includes within '*arete*' range significantly more widely than moral virtue as that idea is usually understood these days. Further references to the Ross/Urmson transation will be placed parenthetically in the text (to lines of Immanuel Bekker's standard edition of Aristotle's Greek text).

2. The photograph, taken by Linda Rosier, accompanied "Stretching Boundaries to Honor a Diva," by Anthony Tommasini, in the National Edition of the *New York Times* for September, 28, 1996. It evidently did not appear in the full edition of the paper that was archived and microfilmed.

3. Although neither by Ross nor by Terence Irwin, both of whom use "happiness." For a defense of translating *eudaimonia* as "flourishing," see Cooper 1975, 89–90, n. 1.

4. *Oxford English Dictionary*, 2d ed.

5. Here I follow, for example, Cooper 1996. See also Rogers 1993. For the possibly conflicting view that '*to kalon*' refers to the common good, see Irwin 1985.

6. Taylor 1985, 16–21. Taylor contrasts "strong evaluation" with "weak evaluation," saying of weak evaluation that for something to be (weakly) judged good, "it is sufficient that it be desired." However, this probably misses the contrast he has in mind, since critically-informed-desire accounts of evaluation, such as Railton's account of a person's nonmoral good (Railton 1986a), will count as strong evaluation by that criterion. Strong evaluation seems rather to concern what Taylor calls the "worth" of desires, where worth is characterized in terms of such categories as "noble" and "base." When I come to discuss these matters below, I will use 'merit' where Taylor uses 'worth', reserving 'worth' for values to which desires that have merit themselves respond. For an excellent critical discussion of Taylor's distinction, see Flanagan 1991.

7. Within the Kantian view of morality, the difference between merit and worth manifests itself as a distinction between two kinds of respect. (For a discussion of this distinction, see Darwall 1977.) Moral "appraisal respect" is an attitude of moral esteem or admiration for morally good character—the good will—and actions that express it. It is *as of* moral merit. Moral "recognition respect," on the other hand, is as of the dignity of persons—the intrinsic worth any person has simply by virtue of her capacity for moral agency. As a response to merit, moral appraisal respect expresses itself in admiration and emulation. As a response to worth, moral recognition respect shows itself in forms of conduct that expresses appropriate recognition for worth of that distinctive kind, for example, by regulating conduct toward others by principles that they would not reasonably reject.

8. As I think of it, being worthy of care and being worthy of (recognition) respect are different forms of worth. See the discussion of respect and care in Chapter I, pp. 14–16.

9. Cf. Thomas Hurka's view that virtue consists in loving the good (Hurka 1992 and 2001).

10. See here my remarks on sympathy and value at the end of the previous chapter and Velleman 1999.

11. I am indebted to John Broome and Thomas Hurka for very helpful discussion of this point.

12. See, for example, Hurka 1993, 3–23.

13. This seems to be Hurka's view.

14. For the record, however, I do believe that perfectionism fails to appreciate the role that appreciated values play in warranting the claims of self-perfection. What we are prepared to count as perfecting or cultivating ourselves itself depends on what we can see as developing our powers to appreciate values, which cannot in turn reduce to the value of developing those very powers.

15. Unless, of course, it can be fit within a defensible teleological metaphysics.

16. For the idea of a "final" or "more complete" end, of more or less final ends, and of the most final end, see 1097a 24–34. An end is final if it is aimed at for its own sake. One final end is "more final" than another if the first is also appropriately pursued for the sake of the second.

17. As I argue in Chapters I and II.

18. For an elaboration and defense of the idea that distinctive values are normative for distinctive valuing attitudes, see Anderson 1993.

19. For a general noncognitivist account of judgments about what "makes sense" or is rational, see Gibbard 1990. Compare McDowell 1985 and also D'Arms and Jacobson 1994. I also intend my normative claims in this chapter to be neutral as between contending metaethical theories of merit and worth.

20. On the relevance of this distinction to that between consequentialist and nonconsequentialist ethical theories, see Pettit 1991.

21. Again, this idea is elaborated and defended in Anderson 1993, 19–30.

22. For example, on Gibbard's norm-expressivism (in Gibbard 1990), the judgment that something is justified expresses the psychological state of acceptance of a norm warranting that thing. Suppose, as I have suggested, that the judgment that X has merit is understood as the judgment that esteem for X is justified. According to Gibbard's norm-expressivism, then, this judgment will express acceptance of a norm that warrants having esteem for X. The judgment that X has merit will thus express, not an attitude toward X, but an attitude toward an attitude toward X. Cruder noncognitivisms, such as emotivism, do hold that the judgment that something X has value expresses an attitude toward X, but they are problematic as accounts of value *judgment* for this very reason, since one can sincerely say or think that something has value even if one does not currently have a favorable attitude toward it, say, if one knows oneself to be depressed, in a perverse mood, or the like.

23. For a discussion of the way in which attitudes and emotions involve evaluative presentations or "appearances," something's seeming to have a certain value, rather than evaluative belief, see Roberts 1988, Greenspan 1981, and Helm 2001. Here again, I intend to be taking no metaethical stands. I assume, for example, that noncognitivists can proffer some account of judgments about the appreciation of values.

24. Michael Smith makes a similar objection to externalism that it must hold that what explains why the "good and strong-willed" person is motivated to act in accordance with his ethical judgments, even when these undergo radical change, is a *de dicto* desire to do what is right, whereas a morally good person would be moved, rather, by *de re* desires to do the very things he thinks morally good. See Smith 1994, 71–76, 82–83.

25. Aristotelian continence contrasts with *akrasia* or incontinence, acting against one's better judgment. The continent person does what she believes she should, for example, she chooses acts she believes to be noble. What she lacks, and what the virtuous person has, is wholehearted engagement with and enjoyment of noble activity.

26. Aristotle 1985, 37.

27. Another place this distinction shows itself is in athletic competition. There are tennis players who would have better success if what motivated them were less the desire that they win or play a good match or whatever, and more the desire *to* win, play a good match, and so on. Frequently, it is the player who plays with fully engaged enjoyment of the activity itself, and not who simply wants certain propositions about the activity to be true, who is most successful.

28. Here and elsewhere I use the 'as of' construction to stress the way the appearance seems to the person having it. Just as color experience is *as of* an intrinsic color feature, say, the redness of a book, so the experience of esteem involves an "appearance" that is as of an intrinsic "merit feature" of the object of esteem.

29. Compare what James Griffin says about the importance of experiences of "depth" in personal relations to well-being. (See Griffin 1986, 67–68).

30. Just as 'esteem' can refer to an attitude toward merit or one toward worth, so can 'self-esteem.' Regarding the relation between self-esteem as an attitude and its relation toward feelings, I have been helped by discussions with Peter Vranas. See Vranas 2001.

31. As Robin Dillon has pointed out. See Dillon 1997. Dillon actually puts her points in terms of appraisal self-respect (or as she calls it, following Stephen Hudson, "evaluative self-respect"). However, appraisal self-respect is a species of self-esteem, namely, that concerned primarily with moral or moral-like features of the person.

32. Derek Parfit makes a similar claim. See Parfit 1984, 501–502.

33. Brodsky 1995, 21.

34. Sacks 1985.

35. Sacks 1985, 17.

36. Sacks 1985, 18.

37. Moore 1993, 237.

38. Indeed, Moore argued that there is no coherent concept of a person's good. There is only the concept of the absolute goodness of something a person may possess or of his possessing it. Moore famously argued on these grounds that egoism is incoherent (Moore 1993, 150–153).

References

Abramson, Kate. 1997. *Hume's Peculiar Sentiments.* Ph.D. diss., University of Chicago.

Adelman, Pamela K., and R. B. Zajonc. 1989. "Faicla Efference and the Experience of Emotion." *Annual Review of Psychology* 40: 249–280.

Anderson, Elizabeth. 1993. *Value in Ethics and Economics.* Cambridge, MA: Harvard University Press.

Aristotle. 1980. *Nicomachean Ethics.* Trans. W. D. Ross. Revised by J. O. Urmson. New York: Oxford University Press.

———. 1985. *Nicomachean Ethics.* Trans. Terence Irwin. Indianapolis, IN: Hackett Publishing Company.

Baier, Annette. 1994. *Moral Prejudices: Essays on Ethics.* Cambridge, MA: Harvard University Press.

Baron-Cohen. S., A. Leslie, and U. Frith. 1985. "Does the Autistic Child Have a 'Theory of Mind'?" *Cognition* 21: 37–46.

Batson, C. Daniel. 1991. *The Altruism Question: Toward a Social-Psychological Answer.* Hillsdale, NJ: Lawrence Erlbaum Associates, Publishers.

Batson, C. Daniel, and Laura L. Shaw. 1991. "Evidence for Altruism: Toward a Pluralism of Prosocial Motives." *Psychological Inquiry* 2: 107–122.

Bavelas, Janet Beavin, C. R. Lemery, and J. Mullett. 1986. "I Show How You Feel: Motor Mimicry as a Communicative Act." *Journal of Personality and Social Psychology* 50: 322–329.

Bavelas, Janet Beavin, Alex Black, Charles R. Lemery, and Jennifer Mullett. 1987. "Motor Mimicry as Primitive Empathy."

In *Empathy and Its Development.* Ed. Nancy Eisenberg and Judith Strayer. Cambridge: Cambridge University Press.

Blum, Lawrence. 1980. *Friendship, Altruism, and Morality.* Boston: Routledge & Kegan Paul.

Brandt, Richard. 1972. "Rationality, Egoism, and Morality." *The Journal of Philosophy* 69: 681–697.

Brink, David. 1992. "Sidgwick and the Rationale for Rational Egoism." In *Essays on Henry Sidgwick.* Ed. Bart Schultz. Cambridge: Cambridge University Press.

Brodsky, Joseph. 1995. *On Grief and Reason: Essays.* New York: The Noonday Press, Farrar, Straus and Giroux.

Broome, John. 1999. "Normative Requirements." *Ratio* 12: 398–419.

Burroughs, Edgar Rice. 1941. *The Return of Tarzan.* New York: Grosset & Dunlap.

Butterworth, G. E. 1991. "The Ontogeny and Phylogeny of Joint Visual Attention." In *Natural Theories of Mind.* Ed. A. Whiten. Oxford: Basil Blackwell.

Butterworth, G. E., and E. Cochran. 1980. "Towards a Mechanism of Joint Visual Attention in Human Infancy." *International Journal of Behavioral Development* 19: 253–272.

Cooper, John. 1975. *Reason and Human Good in Aristotle.* Cambridge, MA: Harvard University Press.

———. 1996. "Reason, Moral Virtue, and Moral Value." In *Rationality in Greek Thought.* Ed. Michael Frede and Gisela Striker. Oxford: Clarendon Press.

Crisp, Roger. 1990. "Sidgwick and Self-Interest." *Utilitas* 2: 267–280.

Damasio, Antonio R., 1994. *Descartes' Error: Emotion, Reason, and the Human Brain.* New York: Grosset/Putnam.

D'Arms, Justin, and Daniel Jacobson. 1994. "Expressivism, Morality, and the Emotions." *Ethics* 104: 739–763.

Darwall, Stephen. 1977. "Two Kinds of Respect." *Ethics* 88: 36–49.

———. 1983. *Impartial Reason.* Ithaca, NY: Cornell University Press.

———. 1992. "Internalism and Agency." *Philosophical Perspectives* 6: 155–174.

———. 1994. "Hume and the Invention of Utilitarianism." In *Hume and Hume's Connexions.* Ed. M. A. Stewart and J. Wright. Edinburgh: Edinburgh University Press.

———. 1995. *The British Moralists and the Internal 'Ought': 1640–1740.* Cambridge: Cambridge University University Press.

———. 1998. *Philosophical Ethics.* Boulder, CO: Westview Press.

———. 1999. "Sympathetic Liberalism." *Philosophy & Public Affairs* 28: 139–164.

———. 2000. "Normativity and Projection in Hobbes's *Leviathan.*" *The Philosophical Review* 109: 313–347.

———. 2001. "'Because I Want It.'" *Social Philosophy & Policy* 18: 129–153.

Darwin, Charles. 1872. *The Expression of the Emotions in Man and Animals.* New York: D. Applegate.

Davis, Mark H. 1996. *Empathy: A Social Psychological Approach.* Boulder, CO: Westview Press.

Dillon, Robin. 1997. "Self-Respect: Moral, Emotional, Political." *Ethics* 107: 226–249.

Eisenberg, Nancy. 1991. "Values, Sympathy, and Individual Differences: Toward a Pluralism of Factors Influencing Altruism and Empathy." *Psychological Inquiry* 2: 128–131.

Eisenberg, Nancy, and Janet Strayer, eds. 1987. *Empathy and Its Development.* Cambridge: Cambridge University Press.

Ekman, Paul. 1985. *Telling Lies.* New York: W. W. Norton & Company.

———. 1992. "Facial Expressions: New Findings, New Questions." *Psychological Science* 3: 34–38.

Ekman, Paul, and R. J. Davidson. 1993. "Voluntary Smiling Changes Regional Brain Activity." *Psychological Science* 4: 42–45.

Flanagan, Owen J. 1991. "Identity and Strong and Weak Evaluation." In *Identity, Character, and Morality: Essays in Moral Psychology.* Ed. Amelie O. Rorty and Owen J. Flanagan. Cambridge, MA: MIT Press.

Frank, Robert. 1998. *Passions Within Reason: The Strategic Role of the Emotions*. New York: W. W. Norton & Company.

Frankfurt, Harry. 1988. *The Importance of What We Care About*. Cambridge: Cambridge University Press.

Gibbard, Allan. 1990. *Wise Choices, Apt Feelings*. Cambridge, MA: Harvard University Press.

Gilligan, Carol. 1992. *In a Different Voice: Psychological Theory and Women's Development*. Cambridge, MA: Harvard University Press.

Goldman, Alvin I. 1989. "Interpretation Psychologized." *Mind and Language* 4: 161–185.

———. 1992. "In Defense of the Simuluation Theory." *Mind and Language* 7: 104–119.

———. 1993. "Ethics and Cognitive Science." *Ethics* 103: 337–360.

Gordon, Robert M. 1986. "Folk Psychology as Simulation." *Mind and Language* 1: 158–171.

———. 1992. "The Simulation Theory: Objections and Misconceptions." *Mind and Language* 7: 11–34.

———. 1995. "Sympathy, Simulation, and the Impartial Spectator." *Ethics* 105: 727–742.

Greenspan, Patricia. 1975. "Conditional Obligations and Hypothetical Imperatives." *Journal of Philosophy* 72: 259–276.

———. 1981. "Emotions and Evaluations." *Pacific Philosophical Quarterly* 62: 62–63.

Griffin, James. 1977. "Are There Incommensurable Values?" *Philosophy and Public Affairs* 7: 59–79.

———. 1986. *Well-Being: Its Meaning, Measurement, and Moral Importance*. Oxford: Clarendon Press.

Griswold, Charles. 1999. *Adam Smith and the Virtues of Enlightenment*. Cambridge: Cambridge University Press.

Hare, R. M. 1971. "Wanting: Some Pitfalls." In *Agent, Action, and Reason*. Ed. R. Binkley, R. Bronaugh, and A. Marras. Toronto: University of Toronto Press.

———. 1981. *Moral Thinking*. Oxford: Oxford University Press.

Helm, Bennett. W. 2001. *Emotional Reason: Deliberation, Motivation, and the Nature of Value*. Cambridge: Cambridge University Press.

Hoffman, Martin. 1978. "Empathy, Its Development and Prosocial Implications." In *Nebraska Symposium on Motivation*. Ed. C. B. Keasey. Lincoln: University of Nebraska Press.

———. 1981. "Is Altruism Part of Human Nature?" *Journal of Personality and Social Psychology* 40: 121–137.

———. 1984. "Interaction of Affect and Cognition in Empathy." In *Emotions, Cognition, and Behavior*. Ed. C. E. Izard, J. Kagan, and R. B. Zajonc. Cambridge: Cambridge University Press.

———. 1987. "Empathy: Justice and Moral Judgement." In *Empathy and Its Development*. Ed. Nancy Eisenberg and Judith Strayer. Cambridge: Cambridge University Press.

———. 1991. "Is Empathy Altruistic?" *Psychological Inquiry* 2: 132.

Hruschka, Joachim. 1991. "The Greatest Happiness Principle and Other Early German Anticipations of Utilitarian Theory." *Utilitas* 3: 165–177.

Hume, David. 1975 (originally published in 1751). *An Enquiry Concerning the Principles of Morals*. In *Enquiries Concerning Human Understanding and Concerning the Principles of Morals*. Ed. L. A. Selby-Bigge, third ed., with text revised and notes by P. H. Nidditch. Oxford: Clarendon Press.

———. 1978 (originally published in 1739/40). *A Treatise of Human Nature*. Ed. L. A. Selby-Bigge and P. H. Nidditch. Oxford: Clarendon Press.

Hurka, Tom. 1992. "Virtue as Loving the Good." In *The Good Life and Human Good*. Ed. Ellen Frankel Paul, Fred D. Miller, Jr., and Jeffrey Paul. Cambridge: Cambridge University Press.

———. 1993. *Perfectionism*. New York: Oxford University Press.

———. 2001. *Virtue, Vice, and Value*. Oxford: Clarendon Press.

Irwin, T. H. 1985. "Aristotle's Conception of Morality." *Proceedings of the Boston Area Colloquium in Ancient Philosophy* 2: 115–143.

Kahneman, Daniel, and Amos Tversky. 1982. "The Simulation Heuristic." In *Judgment under Undertainty*. Ed. D. Kahneman, P. Slovic, and A. Tversky. Cambridge: Cambridge University Press.

Kant, Immanuel. 1997 (originally published 1785). *Groundwork of the Metaphysics of Morals*. Ed. Mary Gregor. Cambridge: Cambridge University Press.

Kavka, Gregory S. 1986. *Hobbesian Moral and Political Theory*. Princeton, NJ: Princeton University Press.

Korsgaard, Christine. 1986. "Skepticism About Practical Reason." *The Journal of Philosophy* 83: 5–25.

———. 1997. "The Normativity of Instrumental Reason." In *Ethics and Practical Reason*. Ed. Garrett Cullity and Berys Gaut. Oxford: Clarendon Press.

Lewis, David. 1979. "Attitudes *De Dicto* and *De Se*." *The Philosophical Review* 88: 513–543.

Linnert, M. 1982. "Infants' Use of Mothers' Facial Expressions for Regulating Their Own Behavior." Paper presented at the meeting of the Society for Research in Child Development.

Lipps. Theodor. 1903. "Einfühlung, inner Nachamung, und Organempfindaugen." *Archiv für die Gesamte Psychologie* 2: 185–204.

———. 1905. "Das Wissen von Fremden Ichen." *Psychologische Untersuchungen* 4: 694–722.

McDowell, John. 1985. "Values and Secondary Qualities." In *Morality and Objectivity: A Tribute to J. L. Mackie*. Ed. Ted Honerich. London" Routledge & Kegan Paul.

Meltzoff, A. N., and A. K. Moore. 1977. "Imitiation of Facial and Manual Gestures by Human Neonates." *Science* 198: 75–78.

———. 1983. "Newborn Infants Imitate Adult Facial Gestures." *Child Development* 54: 702–709.

Mencius. 1970. *Mencius.* Trans. D. C. Lau. London: Penguin Classics.

Mill, John Stuart. 1979 (originally published 1861). *Utilitarianism.* Ed. George Sher. Indianapolis, IN: Hackett Publishing Co., Inc.

Moore, G. E. 1993 (originally published 1903). *Principia Ethics.* With the preface to a planned, but never published, second edition and other papers. Ed. Thomas Baldwin. Cambridge: Cambridge University Press.

Nagel, Thomas. 1970. *The Possibility of Altruism.* Oxford: Clarendon Press.

———. 1986. *The View from Nowhere.* New York: Oxford University Press.

Noddings, Nell. 1984. *Caring: A Feminine Approach to Ethics and Moral Education.* Berkeley: University of California Press.

Overvold, Mark. 1980. "Self-Interest and the Concept of Self-Sacrifice." *Canadian Journal of Philosophy* 10: 105–118.

Parfit, Derek. 1984. *Reasons and Persons.* Oxford: Clarendon Press.

Pettit, Philip. 1991. "Consequentialism." In *A Companion to Ethics.* Ed. Peter Singer. Oxford: Basil Blackwell.

Railton, Peter. 1986a. "Moral Realism." *The Philosophical Review* 95: 163–207.

———. 1986b. "Facts and Values." *Philosophical Topics* 14: 5–31.

Rawls, John. 1971. *A Theory of Justice.* Cambridge, MA: Harvard University Press.

Roberts, Robert C. 1988. "What an Emotion is: A Sketch." *The Philosophical Review* 97: 183–209.

Rogers, Carl. 1951. *Client-centered Therapy. Its Current Practice, Implications and Theory.* Boston: Houghton Mifflin.

Rogers, Kelly. 1993. "Aristotle's Conception of τὸ Καλὸν." *Ancient Philosophy* 13: 355–371.

Rosati, Connie S. 1995. "Persons, Perspectives, and Full Information Accounts of the Good." *Ethics* 105: 296–325.

Sacks, Oliver. 1985. "The Twins." *New York Review of Books* 32: 16–20.

Scanlon, Thomas. 1998. *What We Owe to Each Other.* Cambridge, MA: Harvard University Press.

Scheffler, Samuel. 1982. *The Rejection of Consequentialism.* Oxford: Clarendon Press.

Scheler, Max. 1954 (originally published in 1913). *The Nature of Sympathy.* Trans. Peter Heath. Hamden, CT: Archon Books.

Shope, Robert K. 1978a. "The Conditional Fallacy in Contemporary Philosophy." *The Journal of Philosophy* 75: 397–413.

———. 1978b. "Rawls, Brandt, and the Definition of Rational Desires." *Canadian Journal of Philosophy* 8: 329–340.

Sidgwick, Henry. 1884. *The Methods of Ethics.* 3d ed. London, Macmillan.

———. 1967 (originally published in 1907). *The Methods of Ethics.* 7th ed. London: Macmillan.

Simner, Mark L. 1971. "Newborn's Response to the Cry of Another Infant." *Developmental Psychology* 5: 136–150.

Skorupski, John. 1999. *Ethical Explorations.* Oxford: Oxford University Press.

Smith, Adam. 1976 (originally published in 1769). *The Theory of Moral Sentiments.* Ed. D. D. Raphael and A. L. Macfie. Indianapolis, IN: Liberty Classics.

Smith, Michael. 1994. *The Moral Problem.* Oxford: Basel Blackwell.

Sobel, David. 1994. "Full Information Accounts of Well-Being." *Ethics* 104: 784–810.

Stocker, Michael, and Elizabeth Hegeman. 1996. *Valuing Feelings.* Cambridge: Cambridge University Press.

Stotland, Ezra. 1969. "Exploratory Studies in Empathy." In *Advances in Experimental Social Psychology.* Ed. L. Berkowitz. Vol. 4. New York: Academic Press.

Strawson, P. F. 1968. "Freedom and Resentment." In *Studies in the Philosophy of Thought and Action.* Oxford: Oxford University Press.

Sumner, L. Wayne. 1995. "The Subjectivity of Welfare." *Ethics* 105: 764–790.

————. 1996. *Welfare, Happiness, and Ethics.* Oxford: Clarendon Press.

Taylor, Charles. 1985. "What is Human Agency?" In *Human Agency and Language: Philosophical Papers I.* Cambridge: Cambridge University Press.

Thompson, R. A. 1987. "Empathy and Emotional Understanding: The Early Development of Empathy." In *Empathy and Its Development.* Ed. Nancy Eisenberg and Judith Strayer. Cambridge: Cambridge University Press.

Titchener, Edward B. 1909. *Elementary Psychology of the Thought Processes.* New York: Macmimllan.

Velleman, J. David. 1988. "Brandt's Definition of 'Good.'" *The Philosophical Review* 97: 353–371.

————. 1996. "The Possibility of Practical Reason." *Ethics* 106: 694–726.

————. 1999. "Love as a Moral Emotion." *Ethics* 109: 338–374.

Vranas, Peter. 2001. *Respect for Persons: An Epistemic and Pragmatic Investigation.* Dissertation, University of Michigan, Ann Arbor.

Williams, Bernard. 1981. "Internal and External Reasons." In *Moral Luck.* Cambridge: Cambridge University Press.

Wispé, Lauren. 1991. *The Psychology of Sympathy.* New York: Plenum Press.

Zajonc, R. B., Sheila T. Murphy, and Marita Inglehart. 1989. "Felling and Facial Efference,: Implications of the Vascular Theory of Emotion." *Psychological Review* 96: 395–416.

Index

care theory of, 8–12, 37, 45–49; vs. interests, 3–4, 23–24, 29, 33–34, 53, 82–83; vs. personal values, 5, 25

Williams, Bernard, 112
worth, 78–80

Zajonc, Robert, 56